IT'S OUR TIME!
(Essential Reading For Every Black Man in America)

(Or His White Woman)

by

the unduly incarcerated - U.S. Miliatry Veteran...
PRINCE MARYLAND

OTHER BOOKS YOU MAY ENJOY BY PRINCE!

From Protest to Policy:
(A Call For Radical Change)

How to Read Women's Feet

White Effort For United Change (Screenplay)

White People's Paper

One Way Out!

Are You Catholic?

Trigger Happy (Screenplay)

White Women, Black Men:
Essential Reading for All White Women
(written under the name - Madison Harris)

(All Books Available at Amazon.com)

****

INTRODUCTION

Hello. My name is Prince Maryland. It is a pleasure to meet you! Thank you for opting in with this paper. Hopefully it will be as transformative for you as it was for me writing it.

Today is January 7, 2021. Protestors stormed the White House yesterday; the Senate confirmed Joe Biden; Georgia voted in (2) democratic senators (one being black - 1st time in history for the state of Georgia) and I finished your paper.

The black senator in Georgia only confirms what I've been saying repeatedly through my writing - This is the BEST time for BLACK MEN in the history of the world! I'm sure you can Google how many blacks were lynched in Georgia from 1800 to present.

Think about it. Georgia is a state where the Klan rallies routinely. I don't know about voter fraud, but I can't see Georgia NOT voting in president Trump for reelection. Something's going on down there because the state has about (10) million people. Out of those (10) million only (30%) or so are black. How did (6.5) million white folks let a black man slip through the cracks and gain office? Is it a harbinger of changing times? You tell me.

What I do know is - If a black man in Georgia can get it in his mind to run for office (taking his life in his own hands), and suddenly <u>win</u> -- Listen folks, hear me well -- EVERY BLACK MAN in America needs to follow suit and get what's his TODAY!

Gentlemen start your engines. We need to hit this thing and hit it FAST before it's too late and they wake up and see black folk is rulin' the world! Did you see Joe Biden's Cabinet? Everything from gay-bobs to Indians. Mark these words, next election - white folks is gonna be wheelin' granny out the nursing homes to vote them Republicans back in office.

We have approximately (4) - well, three and a half (3½) good years brothers to do our thing while no one is looking.

I didn't get a chance to talk about corporations in the paper because I wanted to keep it short and on point. Let me mention here - Please, brother PLEASE - Get you a corporation (not an LLC). Boy here me out now, go to LegalZoom.com and get you a corporation (an S-Corporation) today!

Use part of that FREE stimuls money to invest in yourself before it's too late. Democrats have the House, the Senate and the White House - Checks will be pouring out of Washington like rain from the sky. Every time you look up - More "Help" is on the way. Mitch may need medical attention with Republicans berating the man for NOT approving the $2,000 checks when the Senate had the chance. Trump warned him it was political suicide NOT to approve $2,000 checks and he was right.

What does this mean for us? Brother, get yourself a corporation. You know what? What the hay - I'm going to add a special section to the paper called "Corporations" so I can lace you up proper.

Meanwhile, thanks again for tuning in. Now, if you're a female - especially a white girl 'cause you white girls read anything and everything to stay informed - tell your black man

what you've learned in this paper, please. Sisters do the same.
If the black man won't listen or itsn't absorbing this key knowledge,
so be it. Do it YOURSELF!

Women in general should pick up my book:

From Protest to Policy:
(A Call For Radical Change)
by
Prince Maryland

(available at Amazon.com)

In it I speak directly to women - detailing a radical plan
to put a female in the White House as POTUS in 2024 and I added
a fun movie script called: White Effort For United Change.
I won't spoil the surprise. It's laugh out loud funny (and insightful).

Back to the brothers... I've been in them streets; I've been
just about every walk of life imagineable and I've culled wisdom
from a variety of sources. All of my private education coupled
with pimp pizzaz has led me to see what we as a race have in
front of us today. Boys, It's Our Time! You can sit back and
spend free money for (3½) years if you want too. Me, I'm about
to be the wealthiest black man in history! But, with my wealth,
I'm going to do what a white man taught me years ago. He said,
"When you are climbing the ladder of success, you have to have
one hand stretched out above you to receive help from those higher
than you. You also have to have the other hand stretched down
below you to help those lower than you."

Whoever is reading this...

LET'S CLIMB!

———————————

IT'S OUR TIME!

PREFACE

So, a white man told me about this paper called: Black Men
Don't Read. My buddy downloaded it for me from the internet.
What I read was shockingly true. One part said, If you want to hide
something from a black man - Put it in a book. Can you believe
it? Yet how true is it? Educated black men will read this short
treatise and gain further enlightenment. What you do with that
source of power is up to you.

In a nutshell, we (black men) are living in the greatest
time of opportunity the world has ever known. The auspices of
"freedom" and "inclusion" are in plain view whether they be true
or false. Things for black men are looking up!

Poor George Floyd was like the Black Moses bringing us into
the promised land of inclusion and fair play. Now, you know
and I know nothing has really changed. Take your black butt
down south and mouth off to some white cops and see what happens.
Oh, sure, it looks good and sounds good on TV and in the media.
But we know the truth. We're _still_ black. And - at the end
of the day, being black in America is a bad thing.

The purpose of this paper is to help you (the black man)
take full advantage of this brief moment in time when democrats
are in office; "Conversations" are everywhere (talk is cheap);
Black men have white women on TV commercials (I still can't believe
that one - White men are spinning in their graves!); And it is
(supposedly) "Cool" to be black. Let's get the gettin' 'fore

it's too late an' whitey sees we done took over!

Lord willing, in this paper (I have no notes and am writing completely off the cuff) I will show you step by step moves to do your proverbial "Thing" and get what's yours before it actually is too late.

By the way - Thanks for buying this paper. I appreciate the business. But, more than that, I appreciate the brotherhood. All of my adult life I have wanted to create a semi-secret society of educated brothers who dedicate themselves to furthering the independency and prosperity of our race. I checked out the usual club - Most of my male family members were Free Masons - but none of them resonated with me. I realized it was time to create something new, something fresh.

Dare I digress - All of our REAL leaders are gone. King, "X", the ones willing to lay down their lives for the cause... They are gone. What we have today is pitiful.

I wrote a documentary called: When We Were Black. This film outlines in stark detail HOW we were doing better as a people in the 60s than we are (on a whole) today. Then we focused on things like education, appearance, goals. Then - our hope was to "Be Somebody" remember?

Did Hip-Hop ruin it? Who knows? Did crack disarticulate the growing body? Probably so. Did leaders sell out to the white establishment? You tell me. Compared to the 60s I can say without abatement - As a people - we are more lost today than ever in history. We have no anima or collective body.

It is literally every man, woman and child for himself.

I was born in '65. To this day I can remember walking around the projects of Chicago's South side, carrying my walking stick at age three - Waving to the neighbors and holding conversations with them. Each neighbor looked out for every kid in the projects. They would feed us - inspire us - or whoop that naughty ass collectively. As you know - after they got hold to you it was your parents turn! Oh, the whoopin's were legendary.

People cared. We were in this thing together. You weren't alone. Oh, the beautiful black women. My heart goes out to them.

These were the sisters who built up their man. When I moved to Detroit in the 70s, there was such a deep focus on education and profession - You could not get any parts of the pussy unless you could do three things:

SING

DANCE

GRADUATE HIGH SCHOOL

You think I joking? This is for real brother. These sisters weren't with you unless you had gumption. You had to prove you were doing something with your life. If you were, then they were there to build you up - support your efforts - and soothe you with any and everything they had at their disposal.

We would get our hair braided. This was a secret or esoteric time of assessment. They would listen to your conversation to see if you were "about" something or not. Lord, I miss these girls.

People ask me why I haven't dated a black woman since the
70s and early 80s. I tell them, because the real sisters are
far and few between. The White Woman is the NEW sister.

I'll get blowback from black women. I don't care. Some
of you have vibe from the old school - you are to be applauded.
Today's black woman (again, not all of you) is into Jerry Springer,
The View, The Real, The Talk and everybody else's business but
your own.

Black women in the 60s were strong! How do I know? My mother
was one. I watched her bootstrap her way out of the projects
into the upper middle class via sacrifce, education and hard
work. I never saw the inside of a public school from nursery
school through college. In fact, the only time I entered a public
school was for a regional competition in lily white Sterling
Heights, MI where I won an acting award.

You can't tell me the women then weren't committed to excellence.
The Black Woman was the backbone of the black family. Today,
so many distractions - nails, hair, clothes, shoes, car-take
precedence. Wait, FAKE hair, FAKE nails, knock-off clothes and
purses, over extended credit for cars they can't afford.

Hold it. We (black men) can't blame them. It's our fault
we let our women decompose into some type of primordial goop
King and others would cry their eyes out over.

At some point - black men became completely self engrossed
or "Me, me, mine." Even the bible says, a woman is only the
what? She is the "Reflection" of her man. Ooh! There it is.

Now that I've pissed people off - Let's bring them back to
a place of peace. I'm advocating on behalf of our race, men
and women. We can't have one without the other.

Through this paper's insights and direction - I hope to foster,
if not incite, hope, provision, plans and direction. Folks, we
have a once in a lifetime opportunity to hit it and hit it HARD!

If we act quickly (while no one is looking), we can do like
George Jefferson and finally get our piece of the pie.
Listen to me. Mark my words. Democrats have four years and
it's over! American is almost (70%) white. You are about to
see a mass exodus to the poles in the next presidential election
by white Americans who already feel (those who supported Trump)
slighted.

While these dems are in office and the checks are rolling
of the presses like newspapers - The whole country is distracted,
looking the other way. We slide in - legitmately take as much
as we can grab - and SCOOT! If you've never looted before,
this is your chance to do it legally while nobody's lookin' and
the cops are busy tryin' to keep their union together - (Shh!)
Let's get busy.

# # #

CHAPTER ONE

GETTING STARTED

Every time I watch one of those documentaries on PBS by Gates,
I get this unresolved pit in my stomach. My entire soul wretches
seeing blacks lynched, burned, mangled, whipped, abused and left
for dead. Think about it. We're talking about America, not
some third world country. HOW have whites gotten away with this
heinous behavior?

But, then I turn on the TV (I can't watch more than a hour
or two at most) and I see images of George Floyd's murder.
More black folk getting shot to death or paralyzed while their
abusers go Scott-Free. You tell me - What has changed?

The advent and convergent pace of technology has allowed
wider viewing of the same acts that have plagued America since
its inception - But even with the broader technology, the result
is STILL the same. What changes? Nothing.

So, rather than spend more time protesting and or complaining,
I realized what needs to change... OUR MINDS! We, as a people,
need to change our thinking.

In my book: From Protest to Policy (A Call For Radical Change),
I spell it out clearly what needs to happen. We've been marching
and protesting and TALKING for over what - fifty years? What
has changed? Absolutely nothing.

A cop can kill a black man with inpunity [on camera] because
he knows, nine times out of ten, he will never see the inside
of a jail. Shame.

Our problem - heretofore - is expecting equanimity or parity.
We expect equal treatment under the law. Well, remember, I'm
writing to you from a prison desk on a prison typewriter, sentenced
to triple life because I lost it after learning of my ex-wife's
numerous infidelities, secret abortions and a secret tubaligation
while pretending she could get pregnant. I'm at fault for my
actions. I do not blame her at all. No one can make me "lose"
it today. Turns out I was suffering (undiagnosed) from PTSD,
anxiety and depression from my stint in the military as a combat
medic, along with my tenure for the Detroit Fire Department,
responding to 911 calls.

The point is - no one died. How do you get a triple life
sentence when no one is dead? There was a white man in the county
jail who stabbed his wife (7) times to death. (15) years to
life was his sentence. HOW? I kid you not - a deputy told me
in private "You would have been better off if you killed her."

That's a (100%) true statement from a law enforcement officer.
There is an example of the mind set. They KNOW the law and they
know how to skirt around it better than criminals.

This entitled expectation of equal justice under the law
is a made up fallacy. As the old folks said, "There is no justice...
It's JUST US!"

Once you know the problem you can solve for the answer.
Our first step is to divest our thinking while we retool our
expectations in order to develop a keen plan of attack.
Make no mistake - We can win. But, we have to be smart.

CHAPTER TWO

PLANNING YOUR ATTACK

Now we get to the nitty-gritty. Again, the purpose of the paper is personal empowerment. Ask yourself, what does he have to gain from writing this paper? Obviously I'm not trying to make millions of dollars. At $2.99 I'm practically giving it away for free. So, what is my purpose? What expectations do I have?

The answer is simple. I'm tired of talking. No one is giving you (us) specific tools to overcome these seemingly insurmountable challenges. I've been blessed with laser focus and sharp revelations. Not to mention, as we speak, I HAVE millions of dollars in assets. There is an old saying a white man told me years ago that stuck with me. I say it to learners all the time.

> If you want to know how to get up
> the mountain - Ask the man who goes
> back and forth everyday.

How simple is it? I travel up and down the mountain routinely. Making money _is_ simple. Having a master plan - That is the tricky part. You see, money does you no good without a purpose or a plan. Plus, you need a rudimentary understanding of what money does, or rather, what it is designed to do.

Years ago I read a book called: Rich Dad, Poor Dad. I recently came across it again. The author says something to the affect of, what is the difference between a rich man who gets one dollar and a poor man who gets the same dollar?

I'll just say it like it is... What's the difference between
a black with money and a white man with money? The difference
is - The white man says HOW can I make this dollar work for me?
The brother says, "What can I get with this dollar?"

    After we came up - I spent time in yatch clubs. I became
a member of the Broadway Optimist Club. Many of you have never
heard tell of an "Optimist Club?" This is that secret lily white
stuff. Mm, hmm.

    Point being - Many older white men took a liking to me.
They would set me down and counsel me on money. One man in particular
I can't forget said, Son, do you want to be wealthy like me one
day? Immediately I said YES! He said, "Remember these words.
IF you want to make it in America you need two things. What
are they? Take a guess."

    I replied, "Money and skill." He laughed. "Good thinking"
he replied, "No. In America, the two things you must have are,
investments and land." Investment portfolios include:

ACTIVE INCOME

PASSIVE INCOME

PORTFOLIO INCOME

    Again, many of you are seeing these secrets for the first time.
I may as well be speaking in a foreign language. Let me interpret.

    ACTIVE INCOME in a nutshell is income you are _actively_ making
from the services you perform. Your paycheck or WAGE is active
income. Tips, commissions or if you and your boy are in business
together, the money that you receive from the venture is active.

PASSIVE INCOME is a bit tricky. Technically it's your involvement in passive ventures like real estate, limited partnerships where you are the limited partner not doing material labor or majority work. However, it covers your LOSSES in these ventures too.

So, let's say you made $100,000 last year but your passive interest in your boy's "Limited Partnership" where he told you bubonic weed was going to sell like hot cakes took a COVID hit 'cause no one could leave the house to go to the weed shop.

Well, whatever losses the company took, split them down the middle between you and your boy (let's say your share was $50,000). Now you can DEDUCT $50,000 from your active income. Are you with me?

Instead of being taxed by the IRS for $100,000 - They are only going to tax you on $50,000. Get it? So, your "losses" actually earned you (passively) $50,000 in deductions.

Again, this is this slick white folks stuff that most blacks never heard of before. If you teach them (as I'm empowering you to do) the whole neighborhood could go to LegalZoom.com, start up a bunch of Limited Liability Companies and each year lessen their income tax burden IF you're picking up what I'm laying down.

You can do this safely for (3) years. Look up NOLOS or "NET OPERATING LOSSES"

Well, $2.99??? What was I thinking? $29.99 for this type of game. No - It's not for me. It's for US. Just Us.

PORTFOLIO INCOME is simply the money your investment portfolio is making. Things like your dividends (payouts from your investment in a company:Like those little "samples" Mom would give of her roast or cooking before serving the complete meal), capital gains and more.

As you can see from this brief overview - Money can do a bunch of stuff black folk have no idea it can do.

I want to tell you about a special income strategy that came to me a few minutes ago. I'm going to put it in its own separate chapter so you don't skip over it. I think I'm on to something BIG for our race.

You have to have an attack plan. What do [you] PLAN on doing with the money you make? Up till now you've been a spend thrift. Those days are gone! Rich people put their money to work and let their money BUY them things they want. Oh, there is so much to share but so little time.

I want to keep this paper under (25) pages so people (black men) will read it. Thankfully a few of you sisters and a gang of you little white girls got hooked on the title and are reading this for your man or for personal posterity. The principals work for anyone.

Who said, He who fails to plan, plans to fail? You MUST have a plan. Thankfully, I am here to help you develop one.

    CAUTION: There is no such thing as easy money! If all you're
            doing is trying to get rich - It won't work. People
            who make sustainable cash, offer a service or a product
            needed to further society.

Find a need. Fill it. The capitalist paradigm of supply

and demand holds true today more than ever before. COVID has changed
our culture forever. Mark these words. Now that China knows
how to cripple international economies, there will be another
virus or biological attack. This was simply a trial run.

Let's move on before I say too much. Plan your attack brothers.
Plan your attack.

# # #

CHAPTER THREE

IMMEDIATE INCOME STRATEGY

Okay, this is the strategy I mentioned a moment ago. It came to me as I was eating our little "State" dinner of beans and rice. Those who have enjoyed state-food know what I mean. I heard one man yell - "Put some food on them trays!"

Let's make this quick. It's good.

****

Everyone is getting stimulus checks, yes? Okay - Watch this... (1 million) black people (men, women - white women are welcome to participate since you're officially in the struggly with us) take a paltry $100 - Let me say it again - $100 (one-hundred dollars) and we put it in an escrow account where no one can take it. This account is run as a HEDGE FUND* in perpetuity.

Plain English - If conducted properly, the fund will pay EACH INVESTOR (That's you and I) a quarterly dividend of $100 to $500 per quarter, depending on the fund's performance.

In other words, your little hundred dollars gets you <u>at least</u> $400 a year or $100 each quarter (every three months). Instead of spending up your little hundred dollars on who knows what... You are essentially (I hate to say it like this but it's real) pimping those dollars to bring you back money every three months.

What happens to the hundred million? It keeps working! No one is allowed to touch it. The hedge fund manager gets his/her own pay. If you ask me - It's genius. You could throw your whole check in there and really come-up nicely! In fact, if those same one-million investors put in $1,000 each - The fund is worth $1 billion. Do you know what type of coin a billion dollar hedge fund earns? Apparently not.

But let's look at some real numbers. Okay, blacks represent just about (13%) of America's (320) million population (current 2020 Census notwithstanding). That's roughly (41½ million folk). Are you kidding me?

Now we're talking. We get (20) million or half the population to kick in $1,000 each. You're looking at a $20 billion hedge fund. That means people, you can get a quarterly dividend of $1,000 - $5,000 or $4,000 - $20,000 a year from your initial $1,000 investment. Are you kidding me?

More than the dividend - (20) million people banded together is a powerful constituency politicians will hear and pay heed too!

You want to stop the killings - form a constituency with financial power - Believe it - the killings will stop overnight.

Your $1,000 investment comes BACK to you every (3) months with more??? Fellas, that's real pimpin'!

Ladies, NOW you can go shopping because your money is PAYING for your clothes, shoes, nails, hair, purses, card payment, et al.

# # #

CHAPTER FOUR

WAKE UP!

I'm marveling, still, at this income strategy. Never in
the history of America has a black man been allowed to make money
hand over fist, subverting the status quo. Wake up! If you
cannot see what is in front of you - you are blind.

Obama did realitively little (if anything) for the true "Black
Man" as it were. But, having a black U.S. president for eight
years paved the way for an internal shift reshaping the public
narrative.

As I mentioned earlier - black men on TV commercials are
paired (sexually) with white women. Are you kidding me? You've
seen it. Commercials with the interracial couples waking up
together in bed, yada/yada...

You and I both know, there was a time not long ago when it
was unthinkable to have a black man anywhere NEAR a white woman
on TV.

I'm smiling. I've said this in one of my other books but
it bears repeating. In the 80s while in high school, I watched
General Hospital routinely each and every day. There was a black
man named "Jessie" who was flirting with a Latina girl who looked
almost white. The nation held its breath waiting to see how
far the storyline would go. Would he KISS her? No! Impossible.
They KISSED! Uproar! Controversy rang out like Westminster
chimes. A black man <u>kissed</u> a NON-BLACK woman on TV. I was a

teen back then. All teens who watched the show were hooked on
it. We would call each other on the phone to discuss the day's
events and storylines. This was a big deal.

You'll remember, I attended lily white parochial schools.
In my final high school - Bishop Gallagher (Go Lancers!), there
were (1,500) kids with only (5) blacks. That is about (.3%)
of the school being black. We had (1) Latina. No Asians or
"Others" attended. I'm mixed so I guess I represented the others
but I identify as black (Go Tiger Woods!).

Homecoming dances, and socials were quite interesting.
I had to cull some of the finest sisters from my progressive
upwardly mobile black community to date at these events.
I could sense the little white girls liked me. Everyone was
too afraid to break the color barrier.

HOW - you ask - did I sense the little white girls liked
me? At a party - one of them was sloppy drunk - I love her to
this day - Peggy D. She said forget decorum - The girl grabbed
me in front of (100) people, took me in the bathroom and madeout
furiously with me. To this day I analyze the situation.

I mean, if she was horny - there was a plethora of white
guys to nab. Why the only token black at the party?

One little white girl - Lynnie M. defied societal norms
and just started dating me straight out (in secret); while
another one, Gail M. almost lost her familty inheritance by
dating me semi-openly at school. So, yeah, I know they liked
me; The problem was - society (rich white society) didn't.

What does any of this have to do with you waking up, you
ask? Wake up! You and I know you can have a white girl today.
You've more than likely sallied through quite a few already.
The point is - It's not looked on as taboo anymore.

You still don't get it do you? IF you can date (meaning
screw the daylights out of) white girls openly without rebuke,
then this fake society we're living in HAS to go along with other
things you "should" be able to do, yes?

No one wants to be looked at with the eye of dispersion.
I'm sure I could go up to a uber rich man and his lovely wife
and patently ask him for her hand to inseminate. Not wanting
to be politically incorrect, he probably would ask to watch.

Okay, maybe I'm stretching it a bit (Maybe Not???) but you
get the gist. Fellas; IT'S OUR TIME! Wake up. I can't say
it any more plainly or plainer. We have a PASS to do whatever
we want (within legal parameters) because no one wants to be
the one who shoots us down (no pun intended).

The question is: "What do you want to do?" I'm Christian.
I have a bunch of Muslim friends. These cats are educated gurus.
They pride themselves on knowledge. Yet, Christians and Muslim
brothers in America remain mostly at odds with each other. Why
is this?

My first boxing trainer is Muslim. We worked together to
perfect my technique without hitch. I KNOW it can be done!
Should we tear down these stupid walls and just work together,
we can accomplish feats of such great magnitude, the world will
shudder while the establishment quakes in its boots.

The question remains - What do you want to do? What should
we do (knowing we CAN do whatever we want)?

A really fresh revelation hit me this morning in meditation.
This is the year 2021, yes? We're in the 20s. Look back to
1920 or the "Roaring Twenties" if you will. Blacks were being
shot down in the streets, hung, degraded and ridiculed just like
today. Realitively - nothing has changed for us as far as real
equality.

What has changed is public perception. Fellas, it's "COOL"
to be black! It wasn't cool in the 1920s to be black at all.
The whole struggle - PAY ATTENTION · REAL GAME FORTHCOMING - since
America's inception for the black man has been one thing:
White men did NOT want him putting his big black dick in their
white women. Period!

Imagine you were white in the 1600s and you captured or traded
for African slaves. Your small pecker saw these HUGE giant dicks
swinging like Sinatra in Vegas. You KNOW how horny your white
woman gets and how you can barely satisfy her, right? You KNOW
if these dicks get inside your white women, well, your own manhood
is in serious jeopardy. You may have no white woman at all!

What is your impetus? Keep the black dick out of the white
women - period. It becomes near obssession. You are threatened
by the black cock. Why were so many black men lynched down south?
For interacting with (or falsely accused of interacting with)
"pure" southern "white" women. It was an obssession.
They argued the future of the race was at stake. In truth, they
knew they couldn't compete.

Don't get me wrong. I was an international male dancer and
Gigolo for many, many years. I've seen huge white cocks.
And, believe it or not, some white women prefer smaller to medium
cocks - I was too big. So, no, the white race isn't in jeopardy.

Many white women LOVE the security of the white man's money,
acumen and know-how, but they want that black dick on the side.
I'm digressing (I can't help it).

The point here is elementary. The struggle throughout American
history was keeping the black dick out of the American White
Woman. They lost the battle and the war. The black dick is
too strong. Women (female consumers) dictate the economy.
As in some animal societies, the females select their mates.
American white women have chosen the black dick.

One last time - It is obvious because they are showing black
men together (romantically) with white women on U.S TV commercials.
Once the advertisers gave up - it was all over. Fellas, the
door is officially open. Wake up! We can do anything we want
to do today. The problem is - What do we want to do?

# # #

CHAPTER FIVE

WHAT TO DO?

It has been firmly established - It's Our Time! Now, we move on to drilling into strategies. What do we do with this new found freedom?

First, let me clear something up. Many men think (wrongly); IF I find my self a good woman I can make it. Christians, Muslims and Jews all believe the first five books of the Holy Bible. The first book of Moses called Genesis clearly tells us God created man outside of the garden of Eden. He took the man and PLACED him in the garden and told him - Get to work.

> "And the Lord God planted a garden eastward in Eden;
> and there he put the man whom he had formed."
> Genesis 2:8

> "And the Lord God took the man, and put him into
> the garden of Eden to dress it and to keep it."
> Genesis 2:15

So, we see - God made man to work. There is no such thing as something for nothing. Even in nature we see - those who do not hunt or forage, do not eat. For years black men have wanted something for nothing. We've wanted the females to do the hunting like lions. Forgetting the male lions put their lives on the line protecting the pride.

Our thinking is lopsided. Don't get me wrong. I've been the pimp, the player, the gigolo, the "Kept Man" who only had to throw dick in order to survive and thrive. Stupid! I was Jack stupid. This was conditioning at fault; my wrong

thinking was conditioned in me from an early age. You see, while
I attended and socialized with the lily whites, I would "Hang"
out with older black dudes, hustlers and players, picking up
"Game" from them. "Put yo' foot in a bitch's ass young buck!"
Yeah, well - Triple life later - So much for that so called
sage advice.

"You got to give a ho' a mission young blood." "Work them
ho's like ponies. Put 'em on that track!" It goes on and on.
I soaked it up like a sponge. To me it made sense. Why do hard
labor if I could PMP or Gig-low for the money? Male dancing
ruined any hopes of normalcy for me. Once I SAW the pure power
of the dick and its affect on women - Pff! I jumped off the
grid. 1987 found me in a brand new Pontiac Firebird paid for
by a client (white on red). Money, watches, gold, jewels, pussy,
pads, clothes, daily hair salon and nail appointments, daily
shaves with the hot towels and straight razors with my barber;
this was my way of life.

What good is all of that without a plan? Moreover, what
good is any of it without being able to help my fellow man?
I was physically enabled and spiritually bankrupt. Wow - That's
a quote. Until you not only FIND God but submit to him, life
is meaningless. I'm not thumping the bible over your head.
I'm telling you - man is a spiritual being as well as physical.
How long can you live without eating? How long has it been
since you really fed your spirit? Hmm? Good question, yes?

The first step in this enlightenment journey is identifying God and submitting to HIM. His will (not yours) needs to be first place. Surprisingly, as you do submit and feed your spirit daily like you feed your body, your will and God's will align. You will look up one day and wonder at the STUPID stuff you used to do thinking it was "fun" or "the way." Stupid!

Next, I ask people all the time this question:

> "IF you could do anything in the world you want
> to do - And NOT have to worry about making money
> at it - What would it be?"

I want you to really ponder that question and answer it honestly. Write it down if you have too. Some of you may have answered quickly. For me, it's writing, acting, making movies, art, directing, guiding people towards the truth. All of these tie into one when I say, using my talents God has given me. That is what I would do (am doing) everyday and I'm NOT worrying about making money at any of it.

God has placed dreams and goals and specific talents inside of you, me, every man (and woman) alive. I have no desire to work on car engines. I love getting manicures. Grease, oil, dirt under my nails - Unthinkable, I can't do it. But, I have friends who live for mechanical work. To them I'm the odd one (laugh). Why? Because God didn't place mechanics inside of me. God placed it in them. They are doing what they love to do. I'm doing what I love to do. Are you doing what you love to do? If not, do it. Making the choice is half the battle. God and I (Jesus for me) are partners. God didn't tell Adam what to name the animals did He?

Let's see:

> "And out of the ground the Lord God formed
> every beast of the field, and every fowl
> of the air; and brought them unto Adam
> to see what he would call them: and whatsoever
> Adam called every living creature, that
> was the name thereof."
>
> Genesis 2:19

Would you look at that? Since the beginning of creation, God has only wanted to partner with man and work with him. God has been getting a bad rap. He doesn't want to control you like some puppet. He wants you to do your thing while He helps you. I can dig it.

Some of you may be complaining this is turning into a religious paper. Frankly, you aren't chosen. Many are called, but FEW are chosen. Sorry about your luck; your life is meaningless and will remain so until you smarten up or die.

Sure it sound brash or hard but it's the simple truth. Man cannot live without the assistance of God to any substantial degree of happiness. We are spiritual creatures guided by spiritual forces. Like it or not - you cannot escape the facts. Your spirit (which you cannot see) is receiving information from one of two (2) sources: the devil (and his angels) or God and his Holy angels.

You don't have to believe it. You also don't have to believe in something else you cannot see - Gravity. But don't believe in gravity because you can't see it - That's right. Walk your butt off of a three-story roof. See how far your disbelief gets you.

There are things in this life we can't change. Spiritual
submission is a choice we all have. You do submit to one or
the other because IF you don't follow God, then by default,
you're submitting and subscribed to the devil and his lies.

The good news is you can change right now! Fellas (and any
ladies reading) this is the greatest time in the history of America
for blacks in general - but especially for us - the Black Man!

We can't continue to walk around aimlessly, pleasing ourselves
while our race gets lost more than it is already. We have a
commitment to our kids to make something of this thing we call
life. My son lives in Germany (Thank God!) and is (35) years
old. He's at that age of really deciding what to do with his
life and I'm so happy to be there to help guide him. Many men
in prison are disconnected from their children. I do have one
son somewhere in Northern California his mom gave him up for
adoption while I was in jail. It hurts me not knowing who he
is or what he is becoming. I do know he is black (his mom is
white) and he is in America so he is by nature up against it
in these states.

If black men (we number about [20] million but many are
incarcerated or at-risk) band together we can outdo the pyramids.
Oh, that's right! We HAVE done something together as a people
that stills stands out today???

What is stopping us from doing MORE today than we did then.
Take your time and think about this next question, please.
Name (can you name) (5) things blacks have done as a people
to rival the pyramids over the last (100) years.

The only thing I can see blacks coming together for has been
to march or protest inequality. When is the last time we really
came together to do something major - something substantive?
What have we produced other than collaborations on records?

It's Our Time! But, again - WHAT are we going to do with
it? Why waste this golden opportunity? If you need money,
send me an email with your plan and I'll give you a strategy
for FREE to seed your venture.

Why wait? Here's one for free right now:

Benefits.gov

Go there right now. Take the (5) minute survey and at the
end they will tell you EVERY GRANT available to you at this moment.
I keep telling you - Money is simple to make. It's what you
do with the money that counts.

Meanwhile - I'm at page (25). Man, I want to do this hedge
fund thing. Write me your thoughts. Look, even if the returns
are $1,000 every (6) months - That's $2,000 a year on a $1,000
investment. You've doubled your investment in (12) months.
I was a finance broker in Beverly Hills, CA for Camden Holdings,
Inc. One block west of Rodeo Drive. I know this secret stuff
better than most.

God Bless You and Keep You! Thanks for reading. Contact
me: PrinceMaryland@PriorMilitaryProductions.com And remember...

IT'S OUR TIME!

+

SPECIAL BONUS SECTION

CORPORATIONS

What is a corporation? I studied law and was surprised to
learn from "Black's Law" dictionary (the name has nothing to
do with black people) that a corporation is a legal person.
In other words, this company is an actual individual under the
law. It can sue, be sued, borrow, lend and do everything you and
I do. It is a person with no soul (one commentator said).

The purpose of a corporation is to veil or shield its owner(s)
from personal liability should the company fail. In other words
again, when you put your money into it and it should fail...
No one can sue YOU personally. You are protected behind the
corporate veil. They can only sue the person of the company.

Rich whites were doing this when the Mayflower sailed over.
That's a whole story within itself. Here's the rub, you
can open your own corporation for about a grand with LegalZoom.com
and start your way to financial freedom and economic success.

The best part is - the tax schemes! Your company can buy
your home, car, clothes, et al. If it fails, you can't be sued
personally. You can claim deductions for nearly everything you
do through your company. It's too sweet to be sour.

How would you like $500,000 in corporate credit in less than
(2) years? How would you like $50,000 in corporate credit in
less than a year? It got my attention when I was doing fraudulent
enterprise. I learned that if the company failed, I wasn't
liable for the $50,000 in spent credit. Say what?

Of course, later, after I came to Christ whole-heartedly, I discovered something BETTER than fraud - LEGAL BUSINESS STRATEGEMS. I could (and should) write a book on them.

I told you I was a broker in Beverly Hills, CA one block west of Rodeo Drive on Wilshire Blvd. Have you ever heard of a margin account? Most of you haven't I'm sure. This is a tool employed by wealthy (accredited or sophisticated) investors who "borrow" money to play the stock market.

You can literally (once you qualify) play the market for FREE! The stock market is a scam if you go in as "dumb" money. If you know what you're doing (and) you have coin to participate with - It's a wonderful world of winfalls.

There are so many strategies - but I'm digressing. We're talking about corporations. Here's my thought. Rather than waste precious time trying to teach you (seemingly) complex methodologies - Let's do this...

IF you are serious about wanting to learn and try some of these income strategies, write me: PrinceMaryland@PriorMilitaryProductions com.

Share your thoughts with me on the paper and simply request MORE information on How to Come Up (Legally). I'll give you a hand.

Okay brother (and sister -- white girls included). God Bless You. We'll Talk Later I'm Sure! Read - Proverbs 10:22

ONE MORE THING

I hope this makes it to my editor in time. Guys (and ladies)
I used to LOVE watching the TV series "Columbo" remember it?
Just when they thought he was done, he would say, "One more thing."
What an accent.

Okay. So, as usual, whenever I finish a book or paper, the
next day (or soon after), all sorts of confirmation signs start
appearing.

Today is January 11, 2021. I watched the Super Wild Card
Weekend football Saturday and Sunday. Great games. Thank God
I do not gamble - at all! Cleveland over Big Ben??? Did they
pay him? Don't get me started. Conspiracies are everywhere.
Anyhow, during the commercials - what did I see? Black men coupled
up with white women - plain as day!

One commercial went so far as to have a black man and a white
girl on the phone saying, "We're having a baby!" Are you kidding
me? All restraint is lost - clean gone! You can't slice it
any better than an interracial couple - announcing in prime time
on TV during a play-off game, his big black dick went knee-deep
up in her and she's pregnant with a black child. Hello!

Boys, It's Our Time, bro'. It's Our Flippin' Time.
But WAIT!

You know how I was telling you about (GH) General Hospital?
Please, look up today's episode - do it! 1/11/21

I was busy putting the finishing touches on a masterpiece

drawing in charcoal when SUDDENLY - about 3/4 of the way through
the show - this young black boy (reminiscent of the character
"Jessie" I told you about back in the day) who has a lily white
girlfriend (times they are a changin') - has learned she cheated
on him while he was knocking on death's door in hospital with
a white boy (oh those story lines, eh?).

Somehow, she convinces him to stay with her (I could comment
crassly, but I won't). He tells her he is going to take a shower.
Lo and behold - a WHITE HAND opens the shower door while black
boy is butt naked rinsing off - My heart lept! Jessie all over
again. Would she join him? Would they kiss?

She slid in like a snake - Kissed the man full on the mouth,
then they showed their NAKED BODIES entertwined through opague
glass - preparing to do the DEED!

I knew then and there, this was a clear sign from Heaven
and I MUST include one more thing to convince the naysayers,
finally, once and for all - IT'S OUR TIME!

Look, you don't have to be smart or slick or savvy. Just
be ALIVE. Lean on your boy "P" - I'll help you navigate this
nonsense.

Trump lost his mind and went out (is going out) with a bang.
Twitter suspended him (is that even possible?) his own people
are turning on him and Biden is a puppet. NAACP, ACLU and any
other leftsided group with initials are pulling his strings.
Listen to me - The man HAS TO come through for black people fast
IF he wants another (4) years followed by Harris in his place.

What am I saying? "What ARE you talkin' about "P"?"
Listen, there are going to be programs like you have never seen
or dreamt of in your natural born lifetime.

I know how to hit this thing. Here's a little secret. Say
you have a business registered with Dun & Bradstreet (Dun & who???).
Don't worry about - let me talk. So, I have a business registered
with D&B too. D&B is like Experian for businesses. They control
your business credit score like FICO but it's called PAYDEX.

Okay, You tell D&B I'm doing great business with you and
I tell D&B you're doing great business with me. Both our credit
scores shoot up! Remember $50,000 credit line? My method will
get you half a mil in less that two (2) years.

What if thousands of black men reading this paper contact
me and we ALL start reporting on each other's businesses? Hello?
Tell you what, Can you say Mercedes? BMW? Sure you can. We
ALL come up the white man's way playing his game our way!

I've said too much. Many of you are plotting little schemes
as you read. Forget it. Lean on your boy! I go up the mountain
everyday. I'll have you in a company paid for home, several
cars and appreciable assets and most of all a PORTFOLIO pimpin'
your paper like it's supposed to do.

Gotta Scoot! One more thing...

                        IT'S OUR TIME!!!

                            # # #

About the Author

Prince Maryland is an enigma. God has blessed him with tons of talent.

More than anything, Prince is a reformed man who spends his days giving back any way he can. Whether through art, writing, music, coaching or sharing Christian counselling - he is a man on a mission to share what God has given him.

Prince was born in Chicago, IL on the famous "South Side" in Cooke County Hospital. Haling from humble beginnings in the Cottage Grove projects - Prince and his single mother relocated to Lansing, MI during his formative years.

As her position increased, his mother (Bishop - Dr. Carol Maryland Harris Williams) kept her boy in the best parochial schools money could buy.

He would excel in sports (scholarship to University of Michigan playing football) and acting (working in community theater with the uber famous Paul Feig [Bridesmaids, The Spy]) in a company similar to The Groundlings.

Prince opted for the military where he became a Combat Medical Specialist. Unfortunately, his very first patient was the unit's base chaplain who died in Prince's hands. This incident would go on to haunt him most of his adult life. Undiagnosed with PTSD, depression and anxiety the normal world lost its allure.

He sank into the underground society of players and hustlers. Prince travelled the globe as an international male dancer/choreographer. This secret knowledge of women naturally led him into the tawdry, meretricious world of gigolos, pimps and panderers where he once again excelled.

With the underground comes either prison or death. Thankfully he was spared the latter. Having been the first black FBI agent on the cult classic "The X-Files" in British Columbia, Canada where his player life led him - CA has no love for black men. He was quickly jailed for illegal drug sales.

A brief renaissance saw him land back in the real world as a stock broker in Beverly Hills, eventually becoming a TV and motion picture producer (like most elevated con men become).

Tragically he met the wrong woman online - reverted back to his pimp hand ways and landed a triple life sentence (though no one is dead - Only in CA - No LOVE for blacks).

After extensive (professional) therapy and a strong spiritual awakening - Prince is the man he is today. From prison he has written (130 plus) commercial screenplays - one of which made it to CANNES in France and was optioned. He founded Prior Military Productions, Inc. with his long time friend Joanne - creating a powerful documentary (go to: www.priormilitaryproductions.com). He credits all of his success to God.

+

PORTRAITS

Enjoy some of Prince's favorites!

Please Take Note: Every BLUE MOON, he will select a picture to memorialize in pencil. Send yours for consideration - email directly to him.
Go to: https://www.jpay.com/PEMessages.aspx
State: CA, Inmate #F86550 and create an account to
Send pix to Prince directly in prison. Thank you.

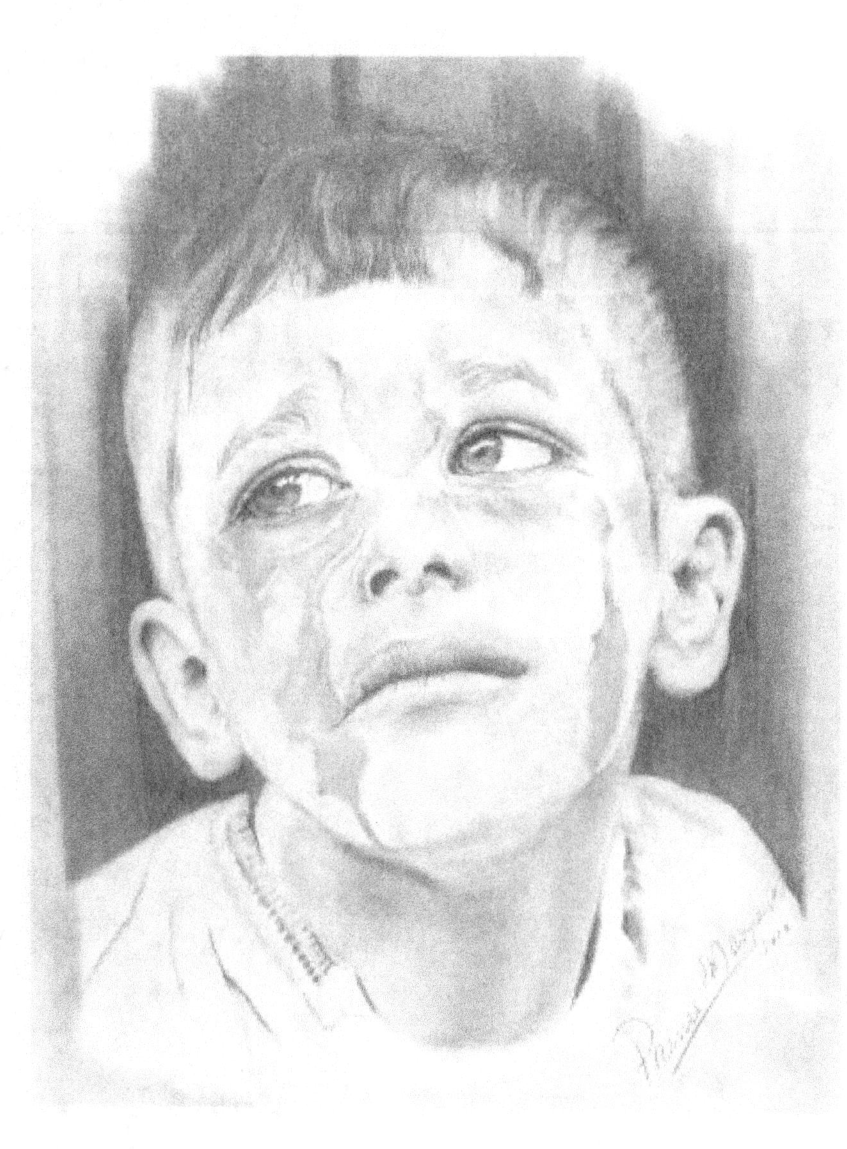

EXTRA SPECIAL BONUS!

Trigger Happy
(full length commercial screenplay)

Currently in development for motion picture production

Trigger Happy

(an original story & screenplay)

by

Prince Maryland

WGA®
PrinceMaryland@PriorMilitary
Productions.com

Trigger Happy

BLACK

(CRAWL) - "The poor man's wisdom is despised, and his
          words are not heard."   Ecclesiastes, 9:16
          ____

SOUND OF FEET RUNNING - HEAVY BREATHING

                    CHIP (OC)
               (running)
          Officer in hot pursuit on foot...
          Suspect, black male, late teens,
          fleeing north on Labrea... Wearing
          dark, hooded jacket, light colored
          pants - five foot nine.

                    BILLY (OC)
               (yells)
          Gun!

SOUND OF GUNFIRE - BARRAGE OF BULLETS

SUDDEN SILENCE

FADE IN:

EXT. STREET (ALLEY) - DAY

Suspect is DOWN - Police Approach (Guns Drawn).

CHIP, 60s, white male - Rumpled inside and out -- BILLY,
20s, white male, Rookie, learning ropes from Chip.

Chip KICKS Dead Body - NO MOVEMENT.

                    CHIP
          You saw a gun kid?

He KICKS Suspect's Hand - CELL PHONE

                    BILLY
          Shit! It looked like a gun, Chip.

                    CHIP
          Mute your camera, hurry up.

Both Men MUTE Body-Cams.

                    CHIP
          Don't worry kid, I'll back you.

Billy is PACING.

                    BILLY
          Chip, I just got married. Carly is
          pregnant. I can't lose--

                    CHIP
          Billy, calm down kid. You did just
          like I taught you. Always shoot
          first. That could be you lyin' there.

                    BILLY
          I don't know... How am I supposed to--

                    CHIP
          Look, when we get to court I'll say--

INT. COURTROOM - DAY

Chip on WITNESS STAND - Testifying.

                    CHIP (CONT'D)
          The suspect turned and faced us in
          a threatening manner. He had an
          unidentifiable object in his hand which
          appeared to be lethal in instrumentation.

                    DEFENSE ATTORNEY
          Please continue officer Kelly.

Courtroom is PACKED with Protestors and Victim's Family members.

                    CHIP
          Fearing for our lives and immediate
          safety we engaged suspect deploying
          live rounds of ammunition until the
          threat was neutralized.

PROSECUTOR STANDS - REPLACING DEFENSE ATTORNEY

                    PROSECUTOR
          Officer Kelly, you emptied your entire
          magazine into the victim, yes?

MURMERS FROM CROWD

                    JUDGE
          Settle down people. This isn't Jerry
          Springer. I will maintain order are
          we clear? The witness may continue.

                    CHIP
               (cool as ice)
          Yes.

                    PROSECUTOR
          And your partner emptied his entire
          magazine into the victim, yes?

FAINT MURMER - JUDGE GIVES THE THE "EYE" - SILENCE

                    CHIP
          I believe he did, yes.

Prosecutor Goes to TABLE - Retreives ITEM - Brandishes
it for the Jury.

                    PROSECUTOR
          And THIS was the lethal looking object,
          an Apple iPhone?

CROWD CAN'T HELP IT - STIR

                    CHIP
          It looked lethal from our vantage point.

                    PROSECUTOR
               (reads file)
          How many black men have you killed
          officer Kelly?

                    DEFENSE ATTORNEY
          Objection! Foundation your honor.

                    JUDGE
          Sustained.

                    PROSECUTOR
          Officer Kelly, have you had occassion
          during your tenure as a Los Angeles
          police officer - How many years on the
          job?

                    CHIP
          Twenty-nine.

                    PROSECUTOR
          During your twenty-nine years have you
          had occassion to use lethal force against
          any African Americans?

CHIP SMILES BROADLY

Chip LOOKS at Jury.

                    CHIP
          Nineteen and counting. All justifiable.
          I keep you safe and sound.

GALLERY MAY ERUPT INTO RIOT

                    JUDGE
          Order. Order!

EXT. COURTHOUSE - DAY

News Gathering Crews Abound.

                    PRETTY FEMALE REPORTER
          Not guilty was the verdict handed down
          today in the Dayshon Johnson case.

Her Voice Trails.

In B.G. People are FIGHTING POLICE!

CUT TO:

VIOLENT IMAGES OF RIOTING - LOOTING - FIRES

FADE:

BLACK

PRESENT DAY - LOS ANGELES

SOUND OF PRISON DOORS OPENING

INT. PRISON VISITING ROOM - DAY

Clean. Federal prison. ROMAN LEWIS, 50s, nice looking,
black male, mid-level independent motion picture/TV producer;

Well dressed - WAITS Patiently for his older brother --
SPARKY, late 60s, short stature, militant views all his
life, short fuse. GUARDS ESCORT Him In.

                    ROMAN
          Sparky.

                    SPARKY
          What's up Roman bread?

UNCOMFORTABLE SILENCE - THEN...

                    ROMAN
          How long are we going to do this
          Sparky? You're the eldest. You
          should be--

                    SPARKY
          Did you pull some strings or not?
          Save the lectures.

                    ROMAN
          I should leave you in here.

                    SPARKY
          What did she say before she died?
          Take care of your brothers.

                    ROMAN
               (points finger)
          You...
               (composes himself)
          Between you and COVID, I don't know
          which one is worse.

BRIEF SILENCE

                    ROMAN (CONT'D)
          I need you to look after Kyle and
          Reggie.

                    SPARKY
          Reggie's a grown ass man. And I ain't
          no babysitter.

                    ROMAN
          You're what I say you are, got it?

TENSION

                    SPARKY
          Whatever. Get me out.

                    ROMAN
          You had the same chances as me.
          How did you--

                    SPARKY
     I didn't go to no Oxford in England.

                    ROMAN
     But you could have. Your I.Q. is
     higher than--

                    SPARKY
     We all got our part to play. Get me
     out an' I'll play mines. Besides, I
     got an idea for all this racial bullshit.

THICK TENSION - MEN STARE AT EACH OTHER LIKE A WESTERN

EXT. CHURCH PARKING LOT - DAY

Very UPSET Roman at (Expensive) CAR with his brothers Sparky
and KYLE, 17, very good-looking, super smart, wants to
fit-in with any crowd.

Kyles is LAUGHING.

                    ROMAN
     What were you thinking Sparky? Have
     you lost your mind?

                    CHURCH LADY #1
     Yo' mama would roll over in her grave
     boy. Shame is what it is.

                    SPARKY
     Check it out gran'ma. You look like
     you need to be doin' some spinnin' your-
     self on one of them bicycles. Lose that
     fat pork chop belly and those hamhock
     thighs.

Church Lady CLUTCHES Her Heart - PASSES OUT. People SURROUND
Her.

Kyle and Sparky are LAUGHING.

                    ROMAN
              (clenched jaw)
     Get in the car, both of you.

TRIES TO LEND ASSISTANCE TO LADY BUT THEY SHOO HIM OFF
(WITH CHOICE - NOT SO RELIGIOUS - WORDS)

INT. ROMAN'S CAR - DAY (TRAVELING)

Sparky in Back Seat.

                    ROMAN (CONT'D)
          What were you thinking? Two for
          one? Is that your plan?

                    KYLE
          It makes perfect sense. For every
          ONE of us they kill, we find their
          kids and kill two of them. Two
          for one. I like it bro'.

                    SPARKY
          Thanks.

                    ROMAN
          Don't be thanking him. And stop
          encouraging him with this militant
          shit.

                    KYLE
          I thought you stopped swearing Pop.

                    ROMAN
          This one brings it out of me.

STARES BRIEFLY AT SPARKY THROUGH REARVIEW MIROR

                    KYLE
          When is Reggie landing?

                    ROMAN
          I'm picking him tomorrow. That's
          another thing. His doctor called
          me. Reggie is suffering from acute
          PTSD, depression and anxiety.

                    SPARKY
          The white man fucked his ass up.
          Nobody told him to go play soldier for
          the man.

                    ROMAN
          He's still our brother and he needs us.
          That means NO weed around the house or
          IN the house at all - both of you.
          Got it?

KYLE SNEAKS LOOK AT SPARKY WHO WINKS - ROMAN IS WATCHING

                    ROMAN (CONT'D)
          One more thing.

                    SPARKY
          Yes, your majesty.

He and Kyle LAUGH it up.

                    ROMAN
          I didn't ask to be some father
          figure. This should be you giving
          orders and looking after things.
          I have a life too.

                    KYLE
          You're good at what you do Pop.

                    SPARKY
          Outta the mouth of babes. Junior's
          right. You're good at what--

                    ROMAN
          Sixteen hours on set. I've got eight
          hours a day to enjoy myself. Part of
          those eight require sleep.

                    SPARKY
          Quit complainin'. You're makin' money
          bro' - In the white man's world. Mad
          respect.

ROMAN IS ALMOST TOUCHED - STARES AT HIS OLDER BROTHER

                    KYLE
          Watch it!

AUTO-BRAKES AVOID COLLISION

                    SPARKY
          You tryin' to get us buried with ma'?

                    ROMAN
          Kyle, you okay?

He NODS.

                    SPARKY
          You okay? Quit worryin' so much bro'.
          It is what it is. Let it happen.

                    ROMAN
          Kyle, I tracked your GPS.

                    KYLE
          You did what? Why?

                    ROMAN
          I pay the bills. Stop going over
          to South Central - I mean it. I know
          you're copping weed. Stop it.

                    KYLE
          I was only--

                    SPARKY
          Nod your head and say yes. Otherwise
          we'll be listenin' to lectures all night
          long.

                    ROMAN
          You're the one who started him on that
          shit.

                    SPARKY
          He had to learn some place. Better me
          than these streets.

                    ROMAN
          Now he's IN these streets-in South
          Central L.A. where the average life
          expectancy of a black kid is--

                    SPARKY
          We got it. No more South Central, right
          Junior?

Kyle Nods his Head.

                    KYLE
          Yes sir.

SNEAKS A WINK AT SPARKY - WHO TELLS HIM (WITH HIS EYES)
TO STRAIGHTEN UP -- ROMAN WATCHES WHOLE EXCHANGE

                    ROMAN
          And Sparky, you're getting a job.

                    SPARKY
          What did I do?

FADE:

INT. POLICE SQUAD ROOM - DAY

Cops Receive DAILY BRIEFING from CAPTAIN WARE, 60s, fed-up Black female - Close to Promotion.

                    CAPTAIN
          It goes without saying...

                    COPS
          Don't kill a black man unless you
          have too.

                    CAPTAIN
          Pay attention knuckleheads. I'm
          minutes away from a white shirt.
               (points)
          Kelly...

                    CHIP
          Can we finish? My donuts are getting
          stale.

White Cops Laugh.

                    CAPTAIN
          You all know about the Kelly rule going
          into effect if we get one more questionable
          shooting.

LOOKS DIRECTLY AT CHIP

                    CHIP
          Hey, I don't care what they say, ain't
          nobody dockin' my pay 'cause I'm doing
          my job.

White Cops Cheer.

                    CAPTAIN
          Shut the fuck up!

DEAD SILENCE

                    CAPTAIN (CONT'D)
          We ALL lose a month's pay indefinitely
          if one of you fuck-ups goes trigger happy.
          I can kiss my promotion goodbye which
          means somebody is on shit patrol at the
          stables - Got it???

LOOKS AROUND AT ALL OF THEM

                        CAPTAIN (CONT'D)
                  Kelly, meet your new rookie --
                  Rusty Adams.

RUSTY, 20s, devastating good-looks, perfect smile, should
be PRINT MODEL instead of cop.

                        KELLY
                  Why are you saddling me with a Ken doll?

Laughter.

                        CAPTAIN
                  The old man doesn't want you riding
                  solo. Adams - Don't learn shit from
                  him. You report back to me if he
                  thinks about shooting a black man,
                  understood?

RUSTY NODS

INT. CHIP'S SQUAD CAR - DAY (TRAVELING)

Chip Driving - Questions Rusty.

                        CHIP
                  Where you from kid? You married?
                  You don't look like you should be a
                  cop. Speak up.

                        RUSTY
                  I--

                        CHIP
                  Shut up! The only thing you need to
                  learn is how to listen. You ride
                  with me you better shoot first and
                  only ask questions IF they survive.
                  Are we clear?

                        RUSTY
                  Yes, sir. My dad was--

                        CHIP
                  Regular fuckin' chatterbox this one.
                  You ever report me to that coon captain
                  and I'll put a bullet in the back of
                  your head with my throwaway piece and
                  blame it on a spook. Are we clear?

No Answer.

                    CHIP (CONT'D)
          Speak up, boy.

                    RUSTY
          Yes sir, I--

                    CHIP
          Shut the fuck up. Regular chatterbox.

PULL INTO MASSAGE PALOR PARKING LOT

                    CHIP (CONT'D)
          Wait here.

                    RUSTY
          What if we get a--

                    CHIP
          Who's trainin' who? Sit your
          ass down and wait.
               (to self)
          Fuckin' rookie.

SOUND OF LOUD GANGSTER RAP MUSIC GETS CLOSER

CHIP TURNS AROUND

                    CHIP (CONT'D)
          What the fuck? It's nine o'clock.

INT. CONVERTIBLE - DAY (TRAVELING)

Several Gangbanger's and Kyle SMOKE WEED Freely - Having
Good Time - Oblivious as they PASS by Squad Car.

SNAKE, 19, lethal looks, black male - RODNEY, 18, equally
deadly, black male.

 Kyle has on Ritzy Private School Uniform (with Tie).

                    KYLE
          Snake, I need to get to school, bro'.

                    SNAKE
          Them white kids can wait. We gon'
          pick up the icky icky. Shit from
          Alaska.

                    RODNEY
          Canada.

                    SNAKE
          Same difference. Shut yo' mouth up
          Rodney. I been smokin' weed since--

LOUD SPEAKER

                    CHIP
               (filter)
          Pull Over!

BOYS PANIC

                    SNAKE
          Oh, shit - Robo-cop!

                    RODNEY
          We got too much dope on us.

                    SNAKE
          Give it to the square. He ain't got
          no record.

                    KYLE
          I can't. My brother will kill--

                    CHIP
               (loud speaker)
          Last warning. Pull Over or else.

                    RODNEY
          That's that trigger happy nigga'
          robo-cop done kilt like twenty nigga's.

                    SNAKE
          Run!

It is OBVIOUS - Snake and the gang members are WELL VERSED
at FLEEING -- Poor Kyle -- Not So Much. Struggles to Get Out.

FINALLY - HOPS OUT LIKE OTHERS - RUNS TOWARDS ALLEY

Rusty GIVES CHASE - Chip SMILES - DRIVES.

EXT. ALLEY - DAY

Kyle is too Fast.

                    RUSTY
          Kid, stop! You don't want to do this.

                    KYLE
                 (running)
            Y'all ain't killing me. I ain't
            going out like George Floyd.

HE ROUNDS CORNER

ONLY TO FIND CHIP WAITING WITH DRAWN WEAPON!

                    CHIP
            Gun!

RUSTY IS SCREAMING

                    RUSTY
            Chip - NO!

SOUND OF GUNFIRE

SLO-MO

KYLE FALLS TO GROUND UNDER HAIL OF BULLETS

SOUND OF BLACK FEMALE GOSPEL SINGER HUMMING TEARFUL SONG

Several People FILM Incident on Their PHONES.

                    RUSTY (CONT'D)
            Why, Chip? Why? He was unarmed.

                    CHIP
            Nobody runs from me. I gotta
            reputation to uphold. Fear is all
            these animals respect. You better
            back me up. Let's get outta here.

Witnesses are getting ANTSY - Vocal Comments Suggest
Imminent VIOLENCE.

                    WITNESS
            They can't kill all of us.

                    WITNESS #2
            Get they ass!

CHIP RUNS TWO OR THREE PEOPLE OVER - ESCAPING

Someone SHOOTS at Squad Car - SHATTERING Back Window.

FADE:

INT. ROMAN'S (STUDIO) OFFICE - DAY

Bungalow on Studio Lot. Quiet, Clean, Nostalgic Feel.

KAREN, 50s or late 40s, exotic white female, mysterious
eyes (good at keeping secrets???), sexy to a fault --
Psychologist - Has one Shoe Off - Listening to Roman.

                    KAREN
          You know this is totally inappropriate?

                    ROMAN
          Come on Karen, you know my crazy
          schedule. I appreciate you coming
          to see me.

                    KAREN
          I don't mean the office visit.

                    ROMAN
          I know what you mean. Come on.
          I'm near crisis again.

SILENCE

                    KAREN
          Go on. I'm referring you to--

                    ROMAN
          I picked Reggie up this morning.
          He's worse than I thought.

                    KAREN
          Is he getting help?

                    ROMAN
          Maybe you could--

                    KAREN
          I'll refer him as well. What about
          Sparky?

                    ROMAN
          You know me too well. He's on my
          last nerve. All he wants to do is
          complain about Black Lives Matter.
          I'm black.

                    KAREN
          So you say.
                    (MORE)

                    KAREN
          You sound more white than most white
          people I know. Continue.

He Gives FRUSTRATED LOOK.

She LICKS Her Pen.

                    ROMAN
          Quit it with the tongue, please.

                    KAREN
          You and your oral fixation...
          What about Sparky?

                    ROMAN
          They asked him for comments at church
          █e yesterday - being polite because
          they knew he was recently released.

                    KAREN
          And?

                    ROMAN
          He told them we should start killing
          cop's kids - Two for every one black
          person. Two for one, can you believe
          it? I was--

                    KAREN
          Protests aren't working. I'm not in
          agreement with your brother, but
          radical change is in order. I was
          reading a new book called from
          Protest to Policy have you read it?

                    ROMAN
          Crisis hello? Not book club.

                    KAREN
          Been a drama king much?

                    ROMAN
          I'm paying you.

                    KAREN
          That's another thing. I can't accept--

Roman is NEAR TEARS.

                    ROMAN
               (emotional)
          What am I supposed to do? I didn't
          ask for any of this. My mom dies
          to COVID? She was healthy as a horse.

KAREN SEES HIS PAIN - HOLDS HER ARMS OUT FOR A HUG

                    KAREN
          Come here. Come here.

LIFTS HIMSELF FROM COUCH - HUGS HER TIGHTLY

COMPOSES HIMSELF QUICKLY

                    ROMAN
          Thanks, I feel--

Karen KISSES Him!

                    KAREN
          Shh. The session is over. I'm
          your girlfriend. Shh.

Make-Out Slowly.

He Glances at Watch

                    ROMAN
          We have twenty minutes.

She is UNDOING Her Top - Kicks Other Shoe Off.

DESK PHONE RINGS

                    KAREN
          Ignore it. I'm ready.

Can't Stop Him.

                    ROMAN
          Could be a problem on set. Sorry.
               (into phone)
          Roman, go... Say that again... Are
          you sure?... His I.D.

SINKS TO FLOOR - KAREN RUSHES OVER

                    KAREN
          What is it honey - Reggie?

SHE TALKS INTO PHONE

                    KAREN (CONT'D)
          This is doctor Karen Seavers...
          He has - I see.

Glances at Distraught Roman on Floor SOBBING MISERABLY.

                    KAREN (CONT'D)
          Where are the remains?... We'll be
          there shortly. Thank you.

COMPLETE SILENCE - WATCH ROMAN GRIEVE

                    ROMAN
          I told him to stay out of South Central.
          Why, Karen - Why?

HE TRIES TO PULL HIMSELF TOGETHER

FALLS BACK ON FLOOR

                    ROMAN (CONT'D)
               (crying hard)
          My mom's dying words she left me
          was take care of your brothers,
          especially Kyle and Reggie.

SUDDENLY HE SCREAMS!

                    ROMAN (CONT'D)
          How much can one man take?(!)

INT. CAPTAIN'S OFFICE - DAY

She is CHEWING OUT Chip and Rusty.

                    CAPTAIN
               (screams)
          How much of this shit can I take?(!)
          I JUST told your sheet wearing ass
          NOT to go killing black people,
          especially UNARMED black men!

                    CHIP
          I have paperwork - Are we finished?

Captain Ware is APOPLECTIC!

GETS IN HIS FACE - CLUTCHING HER HEART

                    CAPTAIN
          (loudly)
     Are we finished? Are we finished?
     I'm not finished but you are you,
     you...

SLINKS DOWN ON DESK - RUSTY HELPS HER UP

                    CAPTAIN (CONT'D)
     Get your hands off of me! Kelly
     turn in your hardware and--

SLUMPS TO FLOOR

RUSTY INTITIATES CPR

                    RUSTY
          (to Chip)
     Call 9-1-1.

                    CHIP
     I ain't callin' shit. Let her die.

LEAVES OFFICE CAUSUALLY - WHILE RUSTY WORKS FEVERISHLY ALONE

INT. ROMAN'S LIVING ROOM - DAY

Sparky and younger brother REGGIE, 30s, black male, clean
cut (military) LOUNGE on SOFA - SMOKING WEED.

TV is ON in B.G.

                    SPARKY
     They ain't got this in Afghanistan
     do they?

                    REGGIE
     Fuck no. My head feels better.

                    SPARKY
     This all they need for you cats comin'
     home with that shit. Canadian hydro.
     I sent Junior to pick up some more from
     his gang'sta boys. He should be back after--
     school -- Hey -- Turn that up. Turn up the
     TV!

News ANCHOR is reporting on Kyle's shooting.

Kyle's STUDENT I.D. picture ON SCREEN.

                    ANCHOR
          We can confirm the latest victim
          in white officer involved shooting
          of black men -- Seventeen year old
          Kyle--

SPARKY SCREAMS!

                    SPARKY
               (screaming)
          No! NO! -- NO!

REGGIE IS FROZEN

Sparky RACES Upstairs.

INT. SPARKY'S ROOM - DAY

Sparky is RUMMAGING Quickly Through Closet LOOKING Desperately
for Something.

Reggie Joins Him.

                    REGGIE
          Spark, we gotta get Roman on--

                    SPARKY
          Got it!

BRANDISHES HAND GUN

                    SPARKY (CONT'D)
          Two for fucking one starting right now,
          you with me?

                    REGGIE
          This ain't like the military. We can't--

                    SPARKY
          Stay yo' scary ass here. Them cops
          about to get dealt with - Proper!

                    REGGIE
          Spark - We can't--

Sparky Fights Emotions.

                    SPARKY
          You wrong, bro'. You can't, but
          I can. They got Junior.

Something REGISTERS With Reggie.

                    REGGIE
               (nods)
          I'm coming with you.

                    ROMAN (OC)
          No you're not. Put the gun down
          Gerald.

Roman with Karen behind him - Holds Out His Hand.

                    ROMAN (CONT'D)
          Give it here.

                    SPARKY
          Who the fuck you supposed to be?
          You got life twisted. I ain't your
          child. And who's this bitch?

                    ROMAN
          Watch your tongue. Give me the gun.
          Gerald - Hand me the--

                    SPARKY
          Quit callin' me Gerald. I ain't answered
          to that name since daddy was alive.
          Move nigga'.

                    ROMAN
          Last time - Hand me the GUN!

SPARKY POINTS WEAPON AT HIS BROTHER

                    SPARKY
          You want the gun? You want the gun?

                    ROMAN
          You lost your damn mind.

                    KAREN
          Why don't we all take a--

                    ROMAN/SPARKY
          Shut up!

22.

KAREN DEMURES IN BACK OF ROMAN

                    ROMAN (CONT'D)
          Put the gun down or I'm gonna
          smack the living daylights out
          of you.

                    SPARKY
          You ain't runnin' shit but your
          mouth - Move out the way.

                    ROMAN
          Or what? You're gonna shoot me?

                    SPARKY
          If I have to - Yeah.

                    ROMAN
          Good luck with that. Do you honestly
          think I'd keep a loaded weapon in
          this house around a known weed-head
          like you?

He INCHES Closer and Closer to Sparky as He Talks.

                    SPARKY
          You're bluffing. I hid this gat years
          ago.

                    ROMAN
          My housecleaner is very thorough.
          Now, give me the gun.

                    SPARKY
          Fuck you.

He AIMS at Roman's LEG - FIRES Pistol!

NOTHING HAPPENS

He PULLS Trigger OVER and OVER - NOTHING...

Roman SNATCHES Gun - SMACKS Sparky SILLY about the HEAD.

                    KAREN
          Roman, stop! You're hurting him.

ROMAN WON'T BE ASSUAGED - CONTINUES BEATING SPARKY'S HEAD

                    ROMAN
              (as he smacks Sparky)
         Hurting him? This little nigga' tried
         to shoot me. I'm gonna beat the dog
         shit out of him once and for all.

Sparky Can't Run - Though he Tries.

                    KAREN
              (to Reggie)
         Do something.

                    REGGIE
         He tried to shoot him.

                    KAREN
         I'm calling the police.

EVERYTHING (EVERYONE) STOPS - ICE COLD SILENCE...

ALL EYES ON KAREN

                    SPARKY
         What did she say? You callin' the
         cops?

                    REGGIE
         Wrong choice of words, lady.

                    ROMAN
              (to Karen)
         Get the fuck out of my house and out
         of my life - NOW! My brother isn't
         cold on the slab and you wanna call
         the people who killed him?

SHE REALIZES HER MISTAKE (TOO LATE)

                    KAREN
         Honey... I--

                    ROMAN
              (yells)
         NOW!

SHE SCURRIES OUT - CRYING

He TURNS His Attention BACK to Sparky who... RUNS!

Reggie SHRUGS. Roman SHAKES His Head in Disbelief.

FADE:

INT. IRISH PUB - NIGHT

Cop shop. All white establishment. Several Cops Buy
Chip Drinks - Slap Him on the Back - Congratulating him.

                    PUB COP
          Congratulations, you killed two
          coons with one stone.

                    PUB COP #2
          Never seen it before today.

                    PUB COP
          Good riddance to the both of them.
               (lifts drink)
          To captain Ware - Wherever she is...
          She won't be harrassing good cops
          anymore.

REST OF PUB CHEER

Rusty ENTERS - LOOKS Around until He Spots Chip.

                    RUSTY
          There you are. I phoned your house.
          Your wife--

                    CHIP
          Has a big fuckin' mouth. Beat it kid.

RUSTY ORDERS DRINK

                    RUSTY
               (to bartender)
          Double Jameson's on ice.

                    CHIP
          Good choice. You gonna back me
          or what?

                    RUSTY
          I already did. I told the board
          I lost visual contact with the
          perp but I distinctly heard you
          announce a weapon's warning.

Chip LOOKS him over carefully.

                    CHIP
          Did they buy it?

                    RUSTY
               (sips drink)
          Why wouldn't they? I'm a good looking
          young rookie cop. What do I have to
          gain from lying?

Chip Considers Him Carefully - Then:

                    CHIP
               (to bartender)
          Give him another one on me.

Rusty Smiles - Lifts His Glass.

Sultry white female, 30s, stacked and packed (front and back),
poured into jeans like a mould - SUZY (Sexy).

Stands Next to Rusty - Sizing Him Up.

                    SUZY
          Hey Chip, this your new partner?

                    CHIP
          Suzy meet Rusty. Rusty, that's
          Suzy. You kids have fun.

                    RUSTY
          Chip, where are you--

SUZY STOPS HIM - PLACING HER HAND ON HIS UPPER INNER THIGH

                    SUZY
               (sultry)
          We don't need him - Do we?

Absently UNBUTTONS a Couple of Buttons On Her Top.

Rusty is STUCK (Staring at Her Seduction).

                    RUSTY
          I guess not. Who are you? I
          haven't seen you around the--

She PLACES Her Index Finger to His Lips.

                    SUZY
          No need to talk. You already closed
          the deal.

EXT. PUB ALLEY - NIGHT

Suzy Has Rusty Against Pub Wall - Languidly SERVICING
Him With Her Mouth - TENSION is Building.

BACK DOOR OPENS

MACK, 20s, white male - Barboy - EMPTIES TRASH.

                    MACK
          Oh - Sorry, Suzy. I didn't know
          You were busy. I didn't see a
          towel on the doorhandle.

                    SUZY
          No worries Mack. Be a dear and
          put a towel up will you?

                    MACK
          Sure thing Suzy, sure.

EXITS

                    RUSTY
          You do this a lot?

                    SUZY
          Practice makes perfect.

                    RUSTY
          Why don't we go back to my place --
          Lose the rats and the smell of urine.

                    SUZY
          You ain't married?

Shakes His Head.

                    SUZY (CONT'D)
          What do you know - That's a first.
          Things is lookin' up...

EYES HIS CROTCH - TINY LAUGH

                    SUZY (CONT'D)
          Lots a things by the look of it.

GRABS HIS HAND - LEADING THE WAY

                    SUZY (CONT'D)
          Stay close behind me. No one will notice.

FADE:

ONE WEEK LATER

INT. TV SET (TALK SHOW) - DAY

Filming in Progress.

Three PUNDITS discuss current EVENTS.

JANE, white, 30s, articulate, pretty, WEARS Sexy Glasses
GLENDA, black, 40s, very attractive face, nice curves
KEVIN, 60s, white male, highly intelligent

MODERATOR is AARON JACOBS, 60s, Jewish.

                    AARON
          Welcome back to This Week Around the
          Nation. I'm Aaron Jacobs with my guest
          panel talking about systemic violence
          among the African American inner city
          or urban communities. Jane, I thought
          after George Floyd things were changing.

                    JANE
          I believe people inherently wanted to
          change. I equate it with shopping around
          for a diet because your doctor told you
          you needed to lose weight but every diet
          you tried didn't fit your lifestyle.

                    KEVIN
          It was an ephemeral notion from the
          outset. Think about it. With the
          coronavirus in full effect, people
          needed a reason to gather.

                    GLENDA
          Kevin is right. While we saw more
          opposite and outside communal support,
          in the end, once the virus resurfaced,
          civil rights took a back seat, again.

                    AARON
          You make a good point Glenda but there
          is a vaccine, several vaccines in fact;
          shouldn't our conversation circle back
          to racial injustice - Especially given
          the latest killing of Kyle Lewis?

                    JANE
          The Kyle Lewis video strikes the same
          visceral cord as watching George Floyd.

                    GLENDA
          I think we're having too many
          conversations and not enough measurable
          action.

                    KEVIN
          We're talking about an embedded culture
          of racial bias. I don't know. Is there
          such an animal as broad equality? If
          so what does it look like?

                    GLENDA
          I think the most immediate question
          that needs answering is - How can a
          man with nineteen murders still be
          walking around on the street free;
          let alone be a cop and carry a gun.

                    AARON
          Has anyone read the book, From Protest
          to Policy?

ALL HANDS GO UP

                    GLENDA
          I fully subscribe to his radical viewpoint
          and his novel outline for legislative change.

                    JANE
          I relate more on his plea to white women
          for support.

                    KEVIN
          His formula is incontrovertible. If
          blacks, white women and 4.5 percent
          of Hispanics band together, they could
          control 53% of the popular vote.

                    AARON
          He's talking about banding together to put
          a white woman in the White House in 2024.
          Kanye watch out.

LAUGHTER

FADE:

BLACK

                    JULIE (OC)
          We're lucky my boss decided to indict.
          Landing a conviction may be tricky.

INT. ASSISTANT DISTRICT ATTORNEY'S OFFICE - DAY

JULIE KENOFF, 50s, covertly attractive, the more you Look
the more you find sexy and appealing - white female - ADA.

CHATS with Roman.

                    ROMAN
          The whole world has seen the videos...
          five of them from various angles.
          My brother never reached for anything.
          His hands were up the whole time.

                    JULIE
          I know mister Lewis, I know.

                    ROMAN
          Call me Roman. I don't know who
          mister Lewis is or where he is for
          that matter.

                    JULIE
          The tapes help us. It's an uphill
          battle.

                    ROMAN
          The man has nineteen murders. How
          is he wearing a badge?

                    JULIE
          I know. I checked into them. All
          justifiable according to the review
          boards. What can I say? We have an
          outdated review system.

                    ROMAN
          Julie, may I call you Julie?

She Nods.

                    ROMAN (CONT'D)
          My family is on the brink of insanity.
          None of us have positive coping skills.
          My brothers are stoned day and night.

                    JULIE
          You've got a year to clean them up.

                    ROMAN
          Why so long?

                    JULIE
          I wish I could do more. Have you
          spoken with a civil attorney about
          wrongful death?

                    ROMAN
          Yes. Money won't bring Kyle back.
          We want justice.

SHE USHERS HIM OUT THROUGH DOOR

                    JULIE
          I know. We'll get there. Patience.

HE EXPLODES

                    ROMAN
          Patience?(!) 500 years isn't long
          enough? Patience?

                    JULIE
          I'm sorry, I have to go.

CLOSES DOOR ON HIM

                    ROMAN
              (to self)
          Patience?

LOOKS AT WATCH

                    ROMAN (CONT'D)
          Fuck it.

EXT/INT. CHIP'S FRONT DOOR - KITCHEN

Rusty KNOCKS on Front Door.

MAGGIE, 60s, white female, soft spoken - very wise, Chip's Wife
ESCORTS him to kitchen.

                    MAGGIE
          Thanks for coming over. He's in the
          back yard moping as usual.

                    RUSTY
          I might have some news to cheer him
          up. We got a new captain. Old school.

                    MAGGIE
          White or black? Please don't say he's
          Mexican, Chip will flip out.

                    RUSTY
          He's white and he's from Georgia.

                    MAGGIE
          He can go back to work?

                    RUSTY
          I have his hardware with me.

MAGGIE GIVE RUSTY A JUICY KISS ON THE MOUTH

                    CHIP (OC)
          Are you gonna fuck her right in
          front of me? What are you doin'
          Maggie?

Maggie CATCHES Herself.

                    MAGGIE
          I'm sorry honey - I couldn't help
          it. He has good news.

                    CHIP
          The only news I wanna hear is I'm
          back on patrol.

Maggie GIVES FLIRTY EYE to Rusty.

                    CHIP (CONT'D)
          Seriously, if you lovebirds wanna do
          it go upstairs.

                    MAGGIE
          I'm baking a pie to celebrate.

After She is Gone...

                    CHIP
          What's up? You didn't like the
          little tart Suzy I set you up with?

RUSTY IS OFFGUARD

Chip Has to Laugh.

MOTIONS WITH HIS HEAD FOR THEM TO GO OUTSIDE

EXT. CHIP'S BACKYARD - DAY

Men SIT on Separate SWINGS - MAGGIE BRINGS BEERS.

                    CHIP (CONT'D)
          Look at that ass. Thirty years
          and I can't keep my eyes off it.

                    MAGGIE
               (walking)
          I heard you.

As Soon is She is Out of EARSHOT.

                    CHIP
          Gimme my shit rookie.

                    RUSTY
          You know?

                    CHIP
          Who's trainin' who? Dave Donovan
          is one of us. I been waiting for
          a break like this for years.

                    RUSTY
          Why am I not surprised. Go back
          to the thing about Suzy?

                    CHIP
          I hear you been holing up with her
          for the past week. She can suck
          buckshot through a rifle, can't she?
          Soft lips.

                    RUSTY
          You had her?

CHIP IS LAUGHING

                    CHIP
          You're dumb as dirt. And to think
          I thought you were I-A undercover.
          You don't know shit, do you? We all
          had her - Join the club kid.

MAGGIE POKES HER HEAD AROUND CORNER

                    MAGGIE
          Honey - Active Shooter on the
          scanner.

                    CHIP
          Where?

                    MAGGIE
          Lincoln high.

                    CHIP
          Let's go check it out kid. I don't
          wanna miss all the fun.

                    RUSTY
          We're off duty.

                    CHIP
          So?

                    MAGGIE
          Make sure he comes back in one piece.

                    CHIP
          I will.

                    MAGGIE
          I was talking to him, not you.

GIVES HUSBAND COY SMILE

FADE:

INT. ROMAN'S KITCHEN - DAY

Sparky at TABLE - EATING HUGE Bowl of Cereal - Lost in Thought.

Reggie SCHLEPS in - LOOKING at Phone in Hand.

                    REGGIE
          You see this?

                    SPARKY
          I can't see shit. These munchies
          got my ass in a--

                    REGGIE
          There's a shooting going on over at
                    (MORE)

                    REGGIE (CONT'D)
          Lincoln high school.

                    SPARKY
          That all white school? What
          happened - Somebody didn't get
          into Yale?

He PICKS Up REMOTE - TURNING TV ON.

TV MONITOR

                    ANCHORWOMAN
          Breaking news with shocking footage.
          We have a live crew at the scene.
          Lori, are you there?

EXT. LINCOLN HIGH SCHOOL - DAY

Preserved. Old White Money. Manicured Lawns. Brick Buildings.

Cop Cars SURROUND Building - Officers with WEAPONS DRAWN.

LORI DAVIS, 20s, fabulous face and body - WEARS Snug Outfit.

                    LORI
          Hi ~~Kathy~~ - Yes, I'm here at Lincoln
          high school, standing about fifty
          yards from where local authorities
          have cordoned off a safe area.

                    ANCHORWOMAN
          Can you tell us what happened? Is
          anyone injured?

                    LORI
          Apparently a lone gunman believed to
          be a student here at Lincoln high,
          entered the building at 10:15 this
          morning and began shooting teachers
          and students at will.

                    ANCHORWOMAN
          Do we know his motivation? Was anyone
          killed?

                    LORI
          Ten people are presumed dead, eleven
          others injured. His motivation is
          unclear at this time.
                    (MORE)

                    LORI (CONT'D)
          Wait! Breaking news.
               (to cameraman)
          See if you can get a shot.
               (to anchorwoman)
          Judy, the gunman has exited the
          building... He is standing in
          front of the school pointing what
          appears to be an attack rifle at
          police.

CUT TO:

EXT. BUILDING (LINCOLN HIGH SCHOOL) - DAY

ALEX ANDERSON, 17, nice looking white male, football star.

HOLDS COPS AT BAY WITH RIFLE

                    ALEX
               (yells)
          Go ahead, kill me! I wanna die.
          Shoot me or I'll shoot you.
               (sobs)
          My life is over. What are you
          waiting for? Kill me!

CHIP HAS ARRIVED ON SCENE WITH RUSTY

                    CHIP
               (to Rusty)
          I know this kid. That's Alex
          Anderson, starting quarterback.

He Addresses Cop on Scene.

                    CHIP (CONT'D)
               (to cop)
          Who's in charge?

                    SCHOOL COP
          Hey Chip. Mike Wilson. Over there.

CHIP IS TELLING OFFICERS NOT TO SHOOT

MIKE WILSON, 70s, lieutenant, white male.

                    MIKE
          Chip, what are you doing here?
          I heard you were suspended.

                    CHIP
          They just reinstated me. Listen
          tell your boys to stand down.
          I know this kid. He plays football.
          Full ride next year to Cal State.
          Something must have happened. Let
          me talk to him.

                    MIKE
          I can't do that. You know the--

                    CHIP
          Two minutes. Just give me two
          minutes with him.

TENSION

                    MIKE
          You got one minute. Go.
              (into prep radio)
          Everyone hold your fire.

EXT. BUILDING - DAY (SCHOOL BUILDING)

Chip APPROACHES Shooter - Hands in the Air.

                    ALEX
          Stay back or I'll shoot!

                    CHIP
          Alex, what's wrong son? I saw you
          last week against Mater Dei. 400
          yards passing... What happened here?

                    ALEX
          Two interceptions... Lexi dumped me.
          I caught her sucking dick behind the
          bleachers and giving tit to two
          black dudes. I'm a laughing stock.

                    CHIP
          Fucking coons. I hate 'em.
          Let's put the gun down and--

ALEX SUDDENLY PLACES RIFLE UNDER HIS CHIN!

                    CHIP (CONT'D)
          Wait... You got to much to live
          for - You're young - We can get
          through this - You obviously went
          temporarily insane. It was a crime
          of passion. Two years in a psych
          ward and you're playin' ball again.

Alex is Listening.

                    ALEX
          Playing ball? How?

                    CHIP
          All this metoo bullshit's got men
          walkin' on eggshells while women
          do whatever the fuck they wanna do.
          You can't even compliment a broad
          without risking a sexual harrassment
          suit. It's a wonder men are gettin'
          laid at all. The gays engineered
          this shit to keep men with men and
          broads with broads. It's a conspiracy.

                    ALEX
          I can play football?

                    CHIP
          Your parents have money. You won't
          see   prison I promise.

                    JUDY/ANCHORWOMAN (OC)
          Can we hear anything they are saying?

                    LORI (OC)
          We're working on it. Wait! It appears
          the off duty officer, Chip Kelly has
          talked the gunman down. He is lowering
          his weapon to the ground.

CHIP HUGS THE YOUNG MAN BEFORE OTHER COPS GAFFLE HIM UP

                    JUDY (OC)
          Lori, do we know if...

HER VOICE TRAILS

INT. ROMAN'S KITCHEN - DAY

Sparking is HOPPING Mad - STOMPS FLOOR!

38.

                    SPARKY
          Did you see that shit? Did you
          see it? The white boy had a AK-47
          attack rifle POINTED at the cops
          an' all they did was TALK??? I'm
          a kill him. If it's the last thing
          I do on this earth I'm a kill that
          man... I'm a kill him!

CUT TO:

FOOTAGE OF RIOTS - LOOTING - MAJOR PROTESTS

                    KEVIN (VO)
          You have to admit, his actions are
          incongruous at best.

                    JANE (VO)
          Convoluted.

                    GLENDA (VO)
          His actions further the narrative
          of dichotomy and inbred inequality due
          to subjective law enforcement.

                    KEVIN (VO)
          Well put.

                    GLENDA (VO)
          I agree.

INT. TOWN HALL - NIGHT

Sparky Behind PODIUM - SPEAKING to Small Gathering.

                    SPARKY
          You saw what they did to my brother.
          Damn shame. He didn't have nothin'
          in his hands - Nothin'!

CROWD STIRS

                    SPAKRY (CONT'D)
          This white boy had a fuckin' AK-47
          semi-automatic attack rifle (which
          I HEAR - is supposed to be illegal)
          pointed right at them!

MORE AGREEMENT

                    SPARKY (CONT'D)
          Some of you is soft. I'm a just
          keep it real an' say it like it is.

                    CROWD MEMBER
          Fuck you little nigga'.

                    SPARKY
          No, fuck you! You wanna get big an'
          bad with me 'cause I'm black. You
          so bad, go gun down some of they kids.
          So what we may go to jail, who cares.
          Three meals a day and some conjugal
          visits is worth makin' them stop killin'
          our people. Two for one!

SOME PEOPLE JOIN HIM

                    CROWD MEMBER
          I ain't goin' to jail for you or
          nobody else. You got me twisted.

                    SPARKY
          Look here jive turkey, you got yo' self
          twisted. They treatin' this funky honky
          like some type a hero for talkin' the
          white boy down. Meanwhile more blacks
          is gettin' killed today than back in
          the 60s. Your jive ass may be next.

CROWD MEMBER RUSHES THE STAGE - PEOPLE STOP HIM

                    SPARKY (CONT'D)
          See. We can kill each other all day
          long. We been killin' each other since
          Africa. Africans STILL killin' each
          other in Africa and over here. How
          is whitey gonna stop killin' us when we
          can't stop killin' ourselves?

CROWD MEMBER SEES THE LOGIC - SETTLES DOWN

Reggie Has Been LISTENING in Back by DOOR.

Something REGISTERS in his Brain.

HE KNOWS WHAT TO DO.

INT. POLICE LOCKER ROOM - DAY

Chip and Rusty DON Uniforms.

Strange SILENCE - No one is SPEAKING to Chip.

                    CHIP
              (to cop)
          Hey, O'Malley, what gives? It's
          as quiet as a morgue in here.

O'MALLEY, 60s, white (Irish) male - Upset.

                    O'MALLEY
          Nice work yesterday with the kid.
          Chip...

                    CHIP
          What? Speak up.

O'Malley LOOKS at Rusty.

                    CHIP (CONT'D)
          He's okay. Go ahead.

O'Malley STEADIES Himself to Deliver News.

                    O'MALLEY
          Chip, the Kelly rule went into effect
          this pay period. Nobody got paid.

                    LOCKER ROOM COP
          Asshole.

                    CHIP
          Watch your mouth buster.

Men Have to BREAK Them Up.

                    O'MALLEY
          Be cool Chip. The captain's on a
          warpath.

                    CHIP
          Donovan is one of us. He can get
          our pay back. Let me go talk to--

                    O'MALLEY
          Donovan ain't here.

CHIP IS CONFUSED

                    CHIP
          What do you mean, Donovan ain't here?
          Who's runnin'--

LOCKER ROOM COP LEAVES

                    LOCKER ROOM COP
               (walking)
          Asshole.

                    CHIP
          Anytime punk, any time.
               (to O'Malley)
          What the fuck is goin' on?

                    O'MALLEY
          Your little stunt with the high
          school kid caused major protests
          and riots.

                    CHIP
          So?

                    O'MALLEY
          The mayor chewed the commissioner's ass.
          It's all about optics.

                    CHIP
          So, who's runnin'--

                    WALTON (OC)
               (deep voice)
          I am. Get your ass in my office, now.

CAPTAIN WALTON - 70s, imposing (large) Black man.

Chip WHISPERS to O'Malley...

                    CHIP
               (whispers)
          What the fuck?

O'Malley SHRUGS.

INT. WALTON'S OFFICE - DAY

He is ALREADY CHEWING ASS - Chip Remains Defiant.

                    WALTON
               (loudly)
     Got it? Your cowboy days are done.
     Ware and I went back to the academy.
     I was her instructor - She was a
     good woman - who, as far as I'm
     concerned - YOU killed.

                    CHIP
     Look, I don't need your speeches.
     All I wanna do is--

                    WALTON
               (smiles)
     All you're gonna do until this trial
     is over is sit your white butt behind
     a desk and answer phones.

                    CHIP
     You can't put me on desk duty. I
     want my union rep.

                    WALTON
     Unlike Ware, my heart is fine.

Hands Him Letter.

                    WALTON (CONT'D)
     Here's a letter from your union rep.

CHIP READS

His Ship is SUNK.

Walton Smiles.

                    WALTON (CONT'D)
               (ultra politely)
     Anything else, officer Kelly?

                    CHIP
     Fuck you. I got some vacation time
     coming. I ain't riding no desk.

                    WALTON
     Allow me to sign off on it ASAP.
     I'm sure the men will be glad to
     know - No further paychecks are
     in jeopardy.

LAUGHS OUT LOUD - CHIP STORMS OUT

Walton YELLS...

                    WALTON (CONT'D)
          Adams! Get your ass in here.

Rusty TRIES to LOOK at Chip as He BRUSHES Past Him BRUSQUELY.

INT. WALTON'S OFFICE - DAY (SECONDS LATER)

Walton CHEWING on MORE ASS.

                    WALTON (CONT'D)
          Do you understand me boy?

                    RUSTY
          Yes sir, I--

                    WALTON
          The next words out of your mouth are
          going to define your career - If you
          have one. Your grandfather was a
          cop. I looked you up. Number two
          in your academy class. You have
          white shirt written all over you.

                    RUSTY
          Thank you sir.

                    WALTON
          Shut up! I not stroking your pecker
          boy. I know Kelly filled your head
          with a bunch of rah-rah nonsense
          about cops sticking together, didn't
          he?

No Answer.

                    WALTON (CONT'D)
          Suit yourself.

CHANGES DIRECTION - SOFTENS

                    WALTON (CONT'D)
          The public has it all wrong. They
          think because we're cops we approve
          of assholes like Kelly. We don't.
          But we can't turn against him because
          he is our brother. Crying shame.
          You're the future, son. These dinosaurs
          are almost gone. Don't let him taint you.

SILENCE

                    WALTON
          (softly)
     What you tell me is completely
     off the record. I want his ass
     and you're going to help me or
     so help me son, you're going
     with him. Understand?

                    RUSTY
     Sir, I--

                    WALTON
     Shut up. Was it a bad shoot yes
     or no? Don't say a word. Nod
     your head if it was good shoot.
     Stand still if it was a bad one.

COPS ALL OVER THE OFFICE ARE WATCHING (THEY CAN'T HEAR)

                    RUSTY
     Sir, I--

                    WALTON
          (yells)
     Just NOD or NOT rookie!

TENSE MOMENT

FADE:

INT. PAWN SHOP - DAY

Reggie in his Military JACKET -- LOOKING at GUNS on COUNTER.

PAWN SHOP OWNER, 70s, jovial, ethnic.

                    PAWN SHOP OWNER
     You are active duty? My boy was
     in the rangers too. Tough unit.
     Will you go special forces?

Reggie IGNORES him - Chooses Weapon.

                    PAWN SHOP OWNER (CONT'D)
     Ah, the desert eagle... Gets the
     job done quickly. I make special
     price for you. Three-fifty, yes?
     No better price in town - I promise.

Reggie Hands Him Bills.

                    REGGIE
          How long do I have to wait.

Owner LOOKS around - LEANS IN.

                    PAWN SHOP OWNER
          Normally you would wait - But you
          are active duty. Take it and go.
          Thank you for your service.

LEANS OVER COUNTER - WHISPERS

                    PAWN SHOP OWNER (CONT'D)
               (whispers)
          If you kill someone with it, throw
          away in the ocean. Shh.

MEN LOCK EYES

INT. ROMAN'S OFFICE - DAY

CINDY, 20s or 30s, cutest (stunning) white female, 5'2"
or lower - attributes for days - Serious CRUSH on her boss.

HANDS Him MESSAGES.

                    CINDY
          I know. I don't get it either?
          It's been like this all day boss.

Roman POURS DRINK from Mini-BAR.

                    ROMAN
          We lost funding for every project?

                    CINDY
          Funding AND distribution. Boss,
          should you be drinking? I thought--

                    ROMAN
          Cindy - This is no time for sobriety.
          Five projects down the drain? Why?
          What did I do?

                    CINDY
          You haven't seen it, have you?

ROMAN DRINKS (TENTATIVELY)

Cindy TURNS COMPUTER MONITOR Towards Him.

ON SCREEN: REGGIE LEADING PROTEST - ALL CHANTING

                         CROWD
              Two for one! Two for one!

BACK TO SCENE

Roman - DRINKS FREELY!

                         CINDY
              Boss? Slow down. The last time
              you drank you said you went on
              a cocaine bender with two es--

                         ROMAN
                    (snaps)
              Shut the fuck up! Can't you see
              it's over? My dream is over.

Her FEELINGS are HURT - She is CLOSE to TEARS.

                         CINDY
              Sir, I was only--

                         ROMAN
              You know how hard it is being black
              in the industry. Black Hollywood
              is what they call us. I worked
              twenty years to get where I am
              Cindy - twenty fucking years, do
              you hear me?

SHE IS CRYING HER EYES OUT

                         ROMAN (CONT'D)
              Tears won't help. It's too late
              for tears.

AWAKENS - SEEING HER PAIN

                         ROMAN (CONT'D)
              I'm sorry. Cindy... Come here.

HOLDS HIS ARMS OUR FOR A HUG

SHE WON'T BUDGE

He Approaches Her.

                  ROMAN (CONT'D)
Can I hug you?

No Answer - Then:

She POURS Herself Into His Arms - Crying.

                  CINDY
What can I do?

                  ROMAN
Nothing. There's nothing we can
do. Hollywood and investors are
the most superstitious animals on
the planet. Maybe I can sell my
library - I don't know.

                  CINDY
What about us?

                  ROMAN
I may have to shut the shingle kid.

THIS CAUSES HER TO CRY HER EYES OUT - HEAVY - MISERABLE SOBS

                  CINDY
But, I love you.

                  ROMAN
We had a good run. I love you
too. Don't tell anyone you worked
for me. You may land another gig.

                  CINDY
Boss?

                  ROMAN
I'm one step away from the pipe.

                  CINDY
Don't talk that way. We can regroup.
I'll stick with you no matter what.
I love you.

                  ROMAN
I know child. I know. This whole--

                  KAREN (OC)
I'm sorry to interrupt.

Karen STANDS - Dressed in Very STRIKING Haute Coutre
(Max Mara Summer Ensemble) - Hair COIFFED to Perfection...
(Dior - Gold Accessories) - VISION of Seduction.

CINDY DISENGAGES QUICKLY

                    ROMAN
          What are you doing here? I thought
          I told you to--

                    KAREN
          Roman, can we talk?

                    CINDY
          I have some errands to run. I'll--

WITHOUT WARNING - ROMAN FRENCH KISSES HER OPENLY IN
FRONT OF KAREN (LONG KISS)

Cindy is STUNNDED After - Hard to Compose Herself.
STUMBLES OUT.

                    KAREN
          Was that necessary? Are you drinking?

                    ROMAN
          You see the drink in my hand bitch.

                    KAREN
          Roman, what's going on. We should
          talk.

                    ROMAN
          When I wanted to talk it was
          unethical you said. I'm tired of
          talking. Talk is cheap. Everybody's
          TALKING. News pundits, presidents,
          the guy at the grocery store -
          Everybody's talking but nothing's
          getting done. My little brother is dead!

                    KAREN
          Roman, honey - Why don't you put the
          glass down and--

HE THROWS GLASS AGAINST WALL

                    ROMAN
          The glass is down - Happy?

DEAD SILENCE - BOTH FROZEN

KAREN EXITS QUIETLY

ROMAN POURS ANOTHER (FRESH) DRINK

                    ROMAN (CONT'D)
          Fucking bitch.

EXT. STUDIO PARKING LOT - DAY

Parking Lot for Bungalow Office.

Karen SEES Cindy SITTING Alone in Car. CATCHES her OFFGUARD
as She TAPS on WINDOW.

                    CINDY
               (rolls window down)
          Karen, I'm sorry. I'm not having
          sex with him. I mean I like him
          and I--

                    KAREN
          I know. Listen, here's my card.
          Keep an eye on him, please. He
          is relapsing hard.

                    CINDY
          He mentioned something about the
          pipe?

                    KAREN
          Alcohol precedes his cocaine smoking
          binges. Please watch him. Call me
          if he self isolates, please.

                    CINDY
          I promise - I will.

                    KAREN
          Thanks. He's lucky to have two women
          who love him.

EXITS SMARTLY - CINDY IN THOUGHT

FADE:

INT. ROMAN'S LIVING ROOM - DAY

Sparky ENTERS Holding LARGE BAG of WEED.

                    SPARKY
          Hey, hey... Brother Reggie, where
          you at? I know we ain't supposed
          to be smokin', but I got this
          gorrilla glue shit guaranteed to
          make your head feel better. Where
          you at? You see me on YouTube?

CONTINUES SEARCHING THROUGH HOME - NO SIGN OF REGGIE

                    SPARKY (CONT'D)
               (to self)
          Must be on a food run. I gotta
          drain the hose.

ENTERS BATHROOM - TALKING TO HIMSELF

                    SPARKY (CONT'D)
          Two for one baby, two for one. I got
          the whole--

FREEZES!

                    SPARKY (CONT'D)
          Reggie!

Reggie Has BLOWN His BRAINS OUT - Sitting On Toilette
in Nothing But His Underwear.

Sparky Bursts into Tears.

                    SPARKY (CONT'D)
          Reggie - No, man - Why? Why bro'?

INT. DINING ROOM - DAY (FLASHBACK)

BABY REGGIE (TODLER) On the RUN From Young Sparky in Nothing
His Diaper - Laughing.

                    YOUNG SPARKY
          Come here little monkey so I can
          change that nasty diaper.

                    BABY REGGIE
          No!

Reggie CATCHES Him - SQUEEZES Him Silly - Both LAUGHING.

END FLASHBACK

INT. ROMAN'S BATHROOM - DAY

Reggie is HUGGING What's Left of Reggie - CRYING.

                    SPARKY (CONT'D)
          Why, man - Why? Come on little brother.
          Breathe man, breathe. You can do it.

SEES PHONE ON SINK

GRABS IT WITH ONE HAND - REGGIE HAS RECORDED SOMETHING

ON SCREEN:

INT. ROMAN'S BATHROOM - DAY (EARLIER)

Reggie ALONE - Pistol in Hand - Phone in Other.

                    REGGIE
          Whoever finds me - Sorry about the
          mess. I can't take this no more.
          They fucked me up over there.
               (beat)
          I was doing security checks in this
          little poor ass village. All the kids
          knew me. But the day before, I guess
          the talian got to their parents.
          Anyway, this little boy blew himself
          up killing five troops. What kind a
          shit is that? How you supposed to win
          a war with kids blowin' they selves up?

HE BEGINS TO CRY

                    REGGIE (CONT'D)
          So, I'm patroling - And outta nowhere,
          this little boy comes runnin' up to me
          with this brown burlap bag in his hand
          screamin' American, American...

BITTER TEARS

                    REGGIE (CONT'D)
          I told him stop - But he kept comin'
          with the bag in his hand. I had to
          do it - I had too. I shot him between
          the eyes. I can still see his face
          every night. He dropped the bag...
          A little puppy came running out.

SETS PHONE ON SINK

                         REGGIE (CONT'D)(OC)
              This is for you kid. I'm sorry.

SOUND OF GUN EXPLODING

END FLASHBACK

INT. ROMAN'S BATHROOM - DAY

Sparky is HUGGING His Dead Brother Silly.

ROCKING BACK AND FORTH WITH HIM

                         SPARKY
              For what man, oil? Oil?
                 (screams)
              I hate these United States!

Leave Him Hugging His Brother - Rocking Back and Forth.

FADE:

BLACK

SOUND OF HEAVY SEX

                         SUZY (OC)
              Fuck -- I'm cumming!

INT. RUSTY'S BEDROOM - DAY

He and Suzy FINISH ROUSING ROUND of SEX in Bed.

She ROLLS Off of Him.

                         SUZY (CONT'D)
              Dammit. What did you do to me?

                         RUSTY
              I should ask you the same question.

                         SUZY
              Let's go again. Get it going.
              Here, I'll help you.

SLIDES DOWN OUT OF FRAME

53.

                    RUSTY
          Suzy, wait... I can't. Let it
          rest. Let's talk.

                    SUZY
                  (giggles)
          Nobody brings me home to talk.
          As a matter of fact - Nobody brings
          me home. Wow. This is the first
          bedroom I've seen in a year.

HAS HER HEAD ON HIS STOMACH

                    RUSTY
          I'm worried about Chip.

                    SUZY
          Chip is fine. He knows the game.

                    RUSTY
          His whole pension is at stake.

                    SUZY
          Thirty years is a long time.

LOOKS Up At Him.

                    SUZY (CONT'D)
          You stayin' in for thirty? I'm
          not.

                    RUSTY
          No way.

                    SUZY
          If he didn't go trigger happy all the
          time he wouldn't have to worry.

                    RUSY
          How well do you know him? Seriously.

She Is Feeling Flirty.

                    SUZY
          Why, you jealous? We fucked a
          couple of times in his car. I
          gave him head behind the bar...
          The usual stuff.

He LOOKS at Her Incredulously.

54.

                    SUZY (CONT'D)
          I know - Suzy the slut is what
          they call me. I don't care.
          I always wanted to be a hooker
          growing up. My mom hooked. As
          a matter of fact, my gran'ma
          hooked too. I learned how to
          trick a man outta his money when
          I was three. I kept candy.

LAUGHS TO HERSELF

                    RUSTY
          But, you're a cop.

                    SUZY
          And a damn good one. I'd do anything
          or anyone for the department. A cop
          saved my life from-- Well look at me
          blabbin' away. Is it ready yet?
          Lemme--

                    RUSTY
          Wait, one more thing.

                    SUZY
          Hurry up. The pussy ain't gonna fuck
          itself.

                    RUSTY
          Has Chip ever told you about his
          bad shoots?

SHE IS IN A FIT OF LAUGHTER

                    SUZY
          Everyone of them is bad. Men say
          stuff to whores and hookers. I
          guess they feel warm and fuzzy inside
          after they pop their nut. He ain't
          never had a good shoot in his life.
          I'm tired of talking - Can we play?

He Smiles - She Goes to Work.

                    SUZY (CONT'D)
          Hello papa!

Leave Them FOOLING Around.

FADE:

BLACK

                    ROMAN (OC)
          I don't believe it. Are you
          negroes smoking weed when I
          told you not too?

INT. ROMAN'S LIVING ROOM - DAY

He Has Bottle of VODKA in Hand LOOKING for His Brothers.

                    ROMAN (CONT'D)
          Where you at Sparky? I can smell
          it clear as day. Don't try to
          hide little nigga'. Gonna be some
          changes up in here. Your ass is
          gettin' a job, you hear me.
               (hollers)
          Where you at?

INT. HALLWAY (ROMAN'S) - DAY

He's Searching Diligently.

WANDERS PAST BATHROOM (OPEN DOOR) - STOPS

SOBERS INSTANTLY

                    ROMAN (CONT'D)
          Reggie?

INT. ROMAN'S BATHROOM - DAY

Roman RUSHES to Reggie's Remains - Sparky PLAYS Cell Phone
Message Over and Over - CATATONIC.

                    ROMAN (CONT'D)
          Sparky? Sparky what happened?
               (yells)
          What happened?(!!!)

SPARKY HANDS PHONE OVER

SOUND OF GUNSHOT

Roman BREAKS DOWN into Gut-Wrenching SOBS.

                    ROMAN (CONT'D)
          First Kyle, now Reggie. Why not
          you. You're the worst one. Why
          couldn't it have been you?

CATATONIC SPARKY SEES GUN ON FLOOR - PICKS IT UP

PUTS IT TO HIS HEAD

                    SPARKY
          It should have been me.

ROMAN SEES HIM

                    ROMAN
          No, Sparky, No! Don't do it, please?

SPARKY IS CONFUSED - POINTS GUN AT ROMAN

(His Head Cocked to One Side Like He's Insane)

                    SPARKY
          I'm the oldest. I should take care
          of you. I'm a take care of you
          Roman bread.

                    ROMAN
          Put the gun down Sparky. Don't
          let Reggie see you do this.

HIS QUICK THINKING SAVES HIS LIFE

                    SPARKY
               (out of it)
          Sorry Reggie, my bad man. I know...
          The cop. Two for one.

LIKE A PROGRAMMED ROBOT HE IS WALKING OUT DOOR

Roman Doesn't Know What to Do.

                    SPARKY (CONT'D)
               (catatonic)
          Two for one.

Roman Dials 9-1-1 (On His Own Phone)

                    911 DISPATCHER (OC)
               (female voice)
          9-1-1, what's your emergency?

                    ROMAN
               (into phone)
          Suicide.

                    911 OPERATOR (OC)
          I'm sorry sir - Are you in distress?

                    ROMAN
          My brother - Reggie - Suicide.

Her Voice TRAILS...

Roman Takes One LAST LOOK at His Brother's Body - LEAVES
His PHONE on FLOOR - Her VOICE Remains AUDIBLE...

                    911 OPERATOR (OC)
          Sir... Sir, are you there? Sir can
          you hear me.

EXT. ROMAN'S HOME - DAY (POV)

Cindy in Her CAR - WATCHES Sparky EXIT (GUN IN HAND)...

MOMENTS LATER - ROMAN GETS INTO HIS VEHICLE

She DIGS Frantically Through Purse - FINDS CARD.

                    CINDY
               (into phone)
          Something's going on. His brother
          has a gun. I hear police sirens
          getting closer... Roman is leaving,
          should I follow him?... It looks
          bad whatever it is... No, he didn't
          look hurt... Okay.

CINDY STARTS CAR - FOLLOWS ROMAN

FADE:

BLACK

                    MAGGIE (OC)
          Thanks for coming over. He's
          been like this for days. Look
          at him. I've never seen him like
          this. I'm worried.

INT. MAGGIE'S KITCHEN - DAY (POV)

She and Rusty EYEBALL - VERY DESPONDENT Chip in Backyard

Absently SWINGING in a World ALL His Own.

                    MAGGIE (CONT'D)
          You don't think he's suicidal,
          do you?

                    RUSTY
          No. Crusty old geezers like him
          have too much hate that's all.

She CONSIDERS HIM For a Moment - WONDERING If She SHOULD...

                    RUSTY (CONT'D)
          Is something wrong?

She Catches Herself.

HOLDS HIS ARM

                    MAGGIE
          We don't have any kids. I don't
          know if it's me or him. We never
          got checked out. We always figured
          when it was time--it would happen.

SOFT TEARS

                    MAGGIE (CONT'D)
          It never did.

Rusty CONSOLES Her.

                    RUSTY
          I get it. I'm like a son to you.

She LOOKS at Him - Confused.

Disengages - Smiles.

                    MAGGIE
                (secretly)
          I don't hardly think of you as a
          son. If I were twenty years younger...
          I'm sorry.
                (laughs)
          No. I was thinking about how lonely
          it is without kids. His birthday is
          coming up - So, I thought I would
          surprise him. Come here.

GRABS HIS HAND - LEADING HIM AWAY

INT. MAGGIE'S DEN - DAY

Nicely furnished. Quiet. Books Abound. Computer in Corner.

MAGGIE ACCESSES COMPUTER

                    MAGGIE (CONT'D)
          I don't know why I'm baring my
          soul to you. I don't have any
          friends. I'm sure you understand.

                    RUSTY
          Being married to him has cost you--

                    MAGGIE
          I love him. I don't love him the
          way I used to love him.

LOOKS AT HIM SIDEWAYS

                    MAGGIE (CONT'D)
          Are you sure you're a rookie? You
          don't carry yourself like a newbie.
          I've been around his trainees for
          twenty years.

STOPS AT COMPUTER - STARES AT HIM

                    MAGGIE (CONT'D)
          You'r I-A aren't you. It's okay.
          You can tell me. I won't tell him.

Rusty Smiles.

                    RUSTY
          I get that a lot. It's the face.
          No. I'm not internal affairs.

                    MAGGIE
          You're not a rookie either. It's
          okay - whatever your secret is.
          We all have secrets.

Goes Back to Computer.

                    MAGGIE (CONT'D)
          Speaking of which - Come here, I
          won't bite you (too hard).

Laughs at Her Own Joke.

                    MAGGIE (CONT'D)
So, I'm thinking... What do you get
the racist biggot who has everything?

                    RUSTY
Misses Kelly.

                    MAGGIE
If you don't call me Maggie...

                    RUSTY
Sorry, Maggie.

                    MAGGIE
You make me feel young again.

KISSES HIM ON THE MOUTH

LAUGHS AFTER

                    MAGGIE (CONT'D)
                  (fans herself)
Can you believe I've never cheated
on Chip all these years?

                    RUSTY
Wow. That's amaz--

                    MAGGIE
It's a lie. I know what he does.
I'm not stupid. Women know these
things. We're like animals. I guess
technically we are animals. I know
he cheats every chance he gets.
I don't know whether to blow up
viagra's head office or invest in
their stock. Those little nasty
pills have put new lead in his pencil.

He Points at Computer.

                    RUSTY
You were showing me something?

                    MAGGIE
See what lack of company does to you?
Anyway - I get mine when and where I
can.
                  (shakes her head)
So, I'm thinking - Why not trace his
roots back to the first biggots in his
shitty family.

                    RUSTY
          A thoughtful gift.

Both Laugh.

                    MAGGIE
          I thought so. Lo and behold...
          He's a heavy sleeper. I swabbed
          his cheeck with a D-N-A sample
          and sent it off to Ancestary dot
          com.

                    RUSTY
          Don't tell me - His roots go back
          to the inception of the klan.

                    MAGGIE
          Speaking of the klan - Did you know
          the N-R-A was originally organized
          and created to keep blacks safe
          from the ku-klux-klan?

                    RUSTY
          No way.

She Nods

                    MAGGIE
          Yep. So many secrets.

EYES HIM KNOWINGLY

HITS A BUTTON ON COMPUTER - WITH FLOURISH

                    MAGGIE (CONT'D)
          Voila!

ON SCREEN:

COLOR PIE CHART - ETHNIC BREAKDOWN

                    RUSTY (OC)
               (looks closer)
          Is that...

                    MAGGIE (OC)
          You see it too?

CHART INDICATES 17.5% AFRICAN AMERICAN

BACK TO SCENE

INT. MAGGIE'S DEN - DAY

                    MAGGIE (CONT'D)
          I was shocked to shit. Excuse
          my potty-mouth.

                    RUSTY
          It's okay. I'm shocked to shit too.
          Are you sure it's him?

                    MAGGIE
          Sweetie, I only live with the one
          man. But, like you, I thought there
          MUST be some kind of mistake.
          You're looking at the second test.

SILENCE

                    MAGGIE (CONT'D)
          I'm a little hungry - Can you stay
          for lunch?

                    RUSTY
          It's my day off. Sure.

                    MAGGIE
          Come here - Look at this...

HITS ANOTHER BUTTON

ON SCREEN:

PICTURE OF BLACK MAN - LEROY JOHNSON (1869).

                    MAGGIE (OC)
          That's him. That's his great grandfather,
          Leroy Johnson.

                    RUSTY (OC)
          You gotta be kidding me. Is this
          for real?

BACK TO SCENE

INT. MAGGIE'S DEN - DAY

She TURNS to Face Him.

                    MAGGIE
          Better than a soap opera, right?
          Apparently papa Leroy's boy hooked
          up with a little Irish chick named
          Molly O'Hara. They disowned her
          because she brought shame to the
          family who go back all the way to--

                    RUSTY
          This is for real? Chip is part
          black?

                    MAGGIE
          Honey, he IS black. In America if
          you have one drop of black blood in
          you, you're black - period.

RUSTY IS STUNNED

She Kisses Him Again.

Laughs to Herself.

                    MAGGIE (CONT'D)
          Nothing wrong with vintage wine.
          Let's eat.

GRABS HIM BY THE HAND

INT. HALLWAY - MAGGIE'S HOME - DAY

Chip has been SECRETLY LISTENING - Darts in Closet to Avoid Them.

Maggie is DRAGGING Rusty By The Hand - Flirting.

Once the COAST is CLEAR - Chip DIPS Into Den.

POV - DOORWAY

Chip LOOKS at Computer in Utter Disbelief.

VISCERAL--SELF CONTAINED REACTION

FADE:

BLACK

64.

SOUND OF SIRENS

SERIES OF SHOTS - NIGHT LIFE IN LOS ANGELES

A)   PEOPLE GOING TO NITE CLUBS
B)   FAMOUS RESTAURANTS
C)   STOCK FOOTAGE OF CELEBS OUT & ABOUT
D)   FANCY CARS - LIMOS

GUNSHOTS

A)   LOOTING
B)   PROTESTS
C)   PEOPLE FIGHTING COPS
D)   SPARKY (HIDDEN IN ALLEY) - SHOOTING AT POLICE

END SERIES

INT. TV (NEWS) STUDIO - NIGHT

Judy at DESK - REPORTING News.

                    JUDY
          Meanwhile in Los Angeles, the
          search continues for a lone gunman
          who reportedly is shooting police
          officers to death. Five officers
          have died - Six others are in
          critical condition. No one knows
          the shooter's identity but officers
          say the perpetrator has been screaming,
          Two for one in reference to him killing
          two officers for every one black life
          taken by police.

     CHANGE ANGLES

                    JUDY (CONT'D)
          The stock market rose today as investors
          anticipate new talks with China over--

HER VOICE TRAILS

INT. HOTEL - NIGHT

Hilton (Suite). Roman and TWO (NEARLY NUDE) Female ESCORTS,
Partying HARD with Champagne and Cocaine (SMOKING) and
Taking TURNS Having SEX.

RHONDA, 30s, gorgeous body, slightly weathered face, white.

LISA, 20s (late teens) - Bright Red Hair - Insatiable
Appetite (for everything).

ROMAN LOOKS HORRIBLE - UNSHAVEN - WILD HAIR

                    LISA
               (having sex)
          There you go daddy. I knew you
          could do it. Rhonda, pass me
          a hit. Put it to my lips as I
          cum. Give one too.
               him

                    ROMAN
          You girls are trying to kill me.

                    RHONDA
          Nuh unh... You're the golden goose
          daddy. We want you to keep laying
          those eggs.

                    LISA
          Gander - male geese are gander.
          I learned that in school when I was--
          Oh shit, I'm cumming - Where's the
          pipe?

Rhonda Positions Pipe in Her Mouth - DEEP HIT...

Lisa Orgasms.

                    LISA (CONT'D)
               (holding breath)
          Come here daddy.

SHOTGUN TOKES SMOKE TO HIM - FOLLOWED BY DEEP FRENCH KISS

                    LISA (CONT'D)
               (to Rhonda)
          Hold his mouth, hurry. Don't let
          him breathe - He's cumming.

ROMAN STRUGGLES HARD - CAN'T BREAK AWAY - ORGASMS

PASSES OUT COLD

                    RHONDA
          Dammit Lisa. Did you kill him?
          What are you kids doin' these days?

                    LISA
          You never seen a blackout toke?

                    RHONDA
          You better hope he ain't dead.

Lisa is RUMMAGING Through His Pants - FINDS WALLET.

                    LISA
          Somehow I get the feelin' he wouldn't
          care if he died.   Oh boy - platinum
          card, yes!

                    RHONDA
          Put that back!

                    LISA
          Don't worry - I'll split it with you.
          We're whores, this is what we do.

DOOR BURSTS OPEN

TWO BURLY SECURITY GUARDS - WEAPONS DRAWN

                    SECURITY
          Freeze!

Followed by CONCERNED Karen.

                    SECURITY (CONT'D)
          Is this him, ma'am.

                    KAREN
          Oh my Lord... Is he dead?

                    RHONDA
          She did it.

                    LISA
          She chocked him to death.   All I
          did was sex.

                    RHONDA
          She made me ch--

ROMAN COMES TOO - BIG BREATH - GULPS AIR

                    ROMAN
          What happened?   I was--

                    KAREN
          Get them out of here, please.

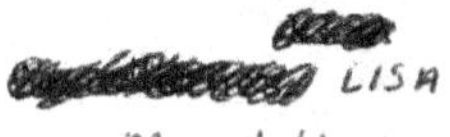

                    SECURITY #2
          You're gonna be wearing jail clothes,
          don't worry.

                    KAREN
          Please, no police.

GOES INTO PURSE - HANDS THEM LARGE BILLS

                    RHONDA
          You must be Karen. He called
          me Karen while he was... You
          know.

                    KAREN
          Get them out of here, please.

GIRLS GRAB CLOTHES

                    KAREN (CONT'D)
          Is that a credit card?

                    LISA
          It's mine. I--

One of the Guards Gives it to Karen.

                    LISA (CONT'D)
          Oh well. If you ever get bored
          and wanna spice things up I
          do married couples. Sunshine
          Escorts. Lisa.

                    RHONDA
                (quickly)
          Rhonda at Juicy Fruit companions.
          Special discount, anytime.

GIRLS ARGUE AS SECURITY HAUL THEM OFF

Awkward Silence.

                    KAREN
          Are you okay?

                    ROMAN
          They could have killed me.

She SITS - GINGERLY - On Bed Next to Him.

PLACES LOVING HAND ON HIS THIGH

                    KAREN
          Honey, what are we doing?
          I'm sorry about the other--

Roman BREAKS DOWN - CRYING - FINDS Her Shoulder.

Karen CRADLES Him Like a BABY.

                    KAREN (CONT'D)
          Let it out baby - Let it all
          out.

                    ROMAN
                   (in tears)
          I lost both of them.

She PATS His Head Lovingly.

                    KAREN
          Shh, I know - I know.

                    ROMAN
          The last thing they said she
          told me was to take care of
          my brothers, especially Kyle
          and Reggie. She knew they
          needed me. I lost both of them.

DISTURBING DISTRESS

She ROCKS Back And Forth With Him IN HER ARMS.

FADE:

INT. MAGGIE'S KITCHEN - DAY

She is HOLDING Rusty's HANDS in Hers As They TALK - LAUGH.

                    MAGGIE
          No, I'm serious - I really can.

                    RUSTY
          To look at at you...

SHAKES HIS HEAD

                    MAGGIE
          I know. I have people fooled. I
          went to Catholic school, with nuns.
          It was a naughty girls' training ground.

                    CHIP (OC)
          I wish you two would fuck and get
          it over with already.

CHIP ENTERS (with) CHIP ON HIS SHOULDER (couldn't resist).

Maggie is UNFAZED - Continues HOLDING Hands.

                    MAGGIE
          You're just jealous. Apparently,
          I've still got it right honey?

                    RUSTY
          I came over to--

                    CHIP
          I don't need cheering up. I'm fine.
          Thanks for stopping by.

                    MAGGIE
               (to Chip)
          I'm heating up the brisket from last--

                    CHIP
               (snaps)
          I don't give a damn.
               (to Rusty)
          Thanks for stopping by.

RUSTY IS CONFUSED - SO IS MAGGIE

This Only Iritates Chip MORE.

                    CHIP (CONT'D)
               (yells)
          Get the fuck outta my house!

                    MAGGIE
          Chip, how dare you--

                    CHIP
          Shut up woman or you're next.

Rusty EXITS Quietly.

Maggie is FUMING MAD.

                    MAGGIE
          Charles, Francis Kelly -- How dare you--

                    CHIP
You wanna fuck him so bad, go live
with him.

                    MAGGIE
What's gotten into you?

                    CHIP
Under my own roof you romance the
dick? MY roof!

                    MAGGIE
What on earth are you talk--

                    CHIP
I heard you. You sounded like
a washed up - wrinkled whore.
He doesn't want your old, used
up--

                    MAGGIE
Watch your tone with me, mister.

                    CHIP
Oh, fuck off.
        (imitates)
Oh Rusty, if I were twenty years
younger I'd suck your dick 'til
it fell off.

                    MAGGIE
I did not say that!

                    CHIP
        (imitates)
Oh, Rusty - Come and taste my vintage
pussy.

SHE HAULS OFF AND SMACKS HIM!

He SMACKS Her Back!

                    MAGGIE
    You hit me.

SHE GETS A HORRIBLE THOUGHT

                    MAGGIE (CONT'D)
What - else did you hear?

                    CHIP
          I heard you telling my personal
          business to a rank stranger, if
          that's what you mean.

                    MAGGIE
          You heard about the--

                    CHIP
          For your information...

STOPS IN MID SENTENCE

She has been married long enough to read his words.

HOLDS HER MOUTH IN HORROR

                    CHIP (CONT'D)
          What's wrong with you?

                    MAGGIE
          Oh, my lord... You knew, didn't you?
          You knew about being--

                    CHIP
          Hush your mouth woman.

                    MAGGIE
          How long have you known Frank?

                    CHIP
          Why are you calling me--

                    MAGGIE
          Francis Kelly - How long have you
          known? If you don't tell me I swear
          I'll call O'Malley's wife and tell
          her ev--

                    CHIP
          Fuckin' chatterbox. Watch it woman.
          You're playin' with fire.

SHE FOLLOWS HIM IN TO LIVING ROOM

INT. CHIP'S LIVING ROOM - DAY

                    CHIP (CONT'D)
          Quit followin' me. Leave me alone.

                    MAGGIE
          Not until you tell me the truth.
          Is this why we never had kids?
          Frank, did you do something to
          yourself to stop me from having
          babies?
                    (mad)
          Did you, bastard!?!

HE IGNORES HER BEST HE CAN

                    MAGGIE (CONT'D)
          If I find out you--

                    CHIP
          Shut the fuck up! You're driving
          me nuts. Yes, I knew - okay?
          I didn't know the specificsuntil you
          start stickin' your nose in everything.

                    MAGGIE
          You knew?

SITS - STUNNED

                    MAGGIE (CONT'D)
          Did you know before you married me?

SILENCE

                    MAGGIE (CONT'D)
          You did, didn't you. That's why we
          didn't fool around on our wedding
          night.
                    (light shines)
          It all makes perfect sense now.
          We didn't have sex until you came
          back from the army overseas in
          Viet Nam. You had it done over
          there, didn't you? Pull it out.
          Let me see it. There's a slight
          scar I never paid any attention too.
          Pull it out Frank!

                    CHIP
          You're out of your fuckin' mind.
          I'm not pulling my pecker out for you
          to--

                    MAGGIE
          I want an annulment. I can get
          it too. Fraud. Our marriage is
          based on a lie.

                    CHIP
          Would you listen to yourself?

                    MAGGIE
          How long have you known?!!!
          The whole truth, now - or so
          help me...

PICKS UP PHONE - DIALS - HE STOPS HER

                    CHIP
          Calm down. Okay. All I know is
          growin' up we used to hear the
          grownups talkin' about dirty Molly
          and the shame she brung the whole
          family takin' up with that darkie.

                    MAGGIE
          From childhood, you knew.

                    CHIP
          I didn't put two and two together
          until right before I met you.

                    MAGGIE
          You knew and you married me anyway?
          You --
               (shakes head)
          Monster.

MOVES TO HOLD HER

SHE CRINGES - BREAKING AWAY FROM HIM

                    MAGGIE (CONT'D)
          Don't touch me. Don't ever touch
          me again.
               (very slowly)
          You're a - nigger. How does it feel?

CHIP IS FIGHTING INTERNALLY WITH EVERYTHING HE HAS TO
MAINTAIN HIS LOOSE GRIP ON REALITY - EYE IS TWITCHING
NERVOUSLY - MAGGIE IS SCARED - BACKS AWAY - INCHES BACKWARD

                    CHIP
               (eerily)
          What did you call me?

Somehow - Through Fear - She STANDS HER GROUND.

                    MAGGIE
          Get used to it. The whole world
          is going to know, Chip Kelly, the
          famous nigger-killer of Greater
          Los Angeles, is the biggest nig--

HE SMACKS THE DAYLIGHTS OUT OF HER

                    MAGGIE (CONT'D)
          You hit me! That was your last
          mistake.

GRABS PHONE

He SMACKS it Out of Her Hand.

                    MAGGIE (CONT'D)
           Leave me alone!

TRIES TO RUN - NOWHERE TO GO

He STANDS In Front of DOOR.

CHIP IS OUTSIDE OF HIS MIND

                    CHIP
               (deliberately)
          I'm going to kill you - then I'm
          going to eat a bullet. Yeah.

                    MAGGIE
          Chip, wait, no - I'm sorry.
               (crying)
          I won't say a word, I promise.
          I don't want an annulment. We'll
          stay married.

                    CHIP
               (crazed)
          I know we will.

                    MAGGIE
          Thank you honey. I'm sorry I--

                    CHIP
          'Till death do us part... Today.

                    MAGGIE
          Chip, I'm sorry. I was only--

                    RUSTY (OC)
          Hello? Guys - I forgot my glasses.
          Is anybody--

MAGGIE SCREAMS HER HEAD OFF

                    MAGGIE
          Help! He's trying to kill me!

CHIP GOES TO ANKLE FOR SPARE GUN

RUSTY ENTERS GUN DRAWN

                    RUSTY
          Hold it Chip. Don't do it pal.

                    CHIP
          I ain't your pal. And you don't
          tell me what to do.

Almost HAS Piece DRAWN.

                    RUSTY
          Stop. You're under arrest.
          Russ Walker - F-B-I.

ALL EYES ON RUSTY

                    CHIP
          I knew something was all wrong
          about you.

PULLS GUN - RUSTY FIRES SHOT - HITTING HIM IN LEG

                    CHIP (CONT'D)
          You shot me?

                    RUSTY
          The next one is through the heart.
          Put it down Chip. Don't be a fool.

HE PUTS GUN - UNDER HIS CHIN!

Maggie is On FIRE.

                    MAGGIE
          Do it! Do it, you black bastard.
          I hate you!

                    RUSTY
          Chip - Don't.

FADE:

BLACK

SOUND OF GUNSHOT

SILENCE

One Month Later

SOUND OF BIRDS SINGING

                    KAREN (OC)
          How do you feel? You look a million
          times better.

EXT. RESIDENTIAL TREATMENT CENTER - DAY

Spacious Grounds. Peaceful.

Roman DOES Look BETTER. WEARS Expensive Track Suit and
Leather (Dior) Open Heel Slippers.

They Sit On PATIO - Sipping TEA.

                    ROMAN
          I needed this. Karen - I can't--

                    KAREN
          There is no need to thank me.
          Besides - I had help.

                    ROMAN
          Cindy. God bless her.

                    KAREN
          You know she's in love with you?

                    ROMAN
          I can't think about women right now.

                    KAREN
          There I go again. I'm sorry.

He TAKES HiS SHADES OFF - STARES AT Her.

SHE Does The Same.

                    ROMAN
          Karen, my mom saw something in me
          I didn't know I had. She saw
          leadership. I remember Sparky
          coming home one day all beat up
          and bleeding. I must have been
          twelve. Kyle wasn't even born
          yet. Reggie was still in diapers.

                    KAREN
          What happened?

                    ROMAN
          A bully at his high school beat
          him up. I had been in boxing
          since nine. I skipped school
          the next day - found the guy and
          beat his ass into the ground.
               (laughs)
          A seventh grader beat a junior's
          ass.

                    KAREN
          Good for you.

                    ROMAN
          No it wasn't. It backfired.
          Sparky wouldn't talk to me.
          I think that's when our relationship
          changed permanently now that I
          think about it. He was embarassed
          his little brother had to stick up
          for him. I've been sticking up for
          everyone ever since.

                    KAREN
          What a memory.

                    ROMAN
          Mom bought me a pie all for myself.
          She told me I did the right thing.

HE GETS EMOTIONAL

KAREN REACHES FOR HIS HAND

                    ROMAN (CONT'D)
          I'm okay. I've been running from
          responsibility. All I have left
          is Reggie. I have to find him.

                    KAREN
          You will baby - You will.

SEES BOOK ON TABLE

                    KAREN (CONT'D)
          What are you reading? Self-help?

Roman Comes TOO from his Thoughts.

HOLDS BOOK UP

ON CAMERA: "FROM PROTEST TO POLICY"

BACK TO SCENE

EXT. PATIO (TREATMENT FACILITY) - DAY (SECONDS LATER)

                    KAREN (CONT'D)
          Oh, you took my advice.

                    ROMAN
          Absolutely. You were right. I
          can't believe his insight. Why
          isn't America talking about this
          man?

                    KAREN
          Well, I guess because--

                    ROMAN
          I'll tell you why. He's in prison.

                    KAREN
          I was going to say the same thing.

                    ROMAN
          The poor man's wisdom is despised,
          and his words not heard.

                    KAREN
          Shakespeare or Francis Bacon?

                    ROMAN
          Try the Holy Bible.

                    KAREN
          Oh?

                    ROMAN
          Karen, he's right. Blacks make up
          about thirteen percent of America's
          population. White women, blacks and
          just (4.5%) of hispanics have the
          majority popular vote. We can put
          a white woman in the white house in
          2024 easily.

                    KAREN
          I know. Not to mention change the
          complexion of the House and Senate.

He HOLDS Her HAND.

                    ROMAN
          Cupcake, forget protests. We've been
          marching since the sixties. One man
          was killed by white cops at Wendy's
          while we were marching.

                    KAREN
          I never thought about it that way.
          You're right.

THERE IS AN EXCITEMENT BETWEEN THEM

                    ROMAN
          We have to change the rules in order
          to change the outcome.

                    KAREN
          You should write it down. I like
          it. Change the rules to change the
          outcome. I really like it.

                    ROMAN
          Listen, I'm going to get something
          from Kyle's wrongful death suit.
          The V-A contacted me - Reggie has me
          down as his beneficiary.

SOMBER MOMENT

                    KAREN
            I'm sorry.

He BREATHES In - DEEP.

                    KAREN (CONT'D)
          It sounds like you have a plan.

                    ROMAN
          I do. I see a movie.

                    KAREN
          A movie?

                    ROMAN
          A movie then a series. America
          has to see a woman in the white
          house under our plan. Our society
          is directly programmed by film and
          TV. Before Obama got elected they
          had black presidents on TV shows
          like (24).

                    KAREN
          I liked that show.

                    ROMAN
          Million' did. That's why they tested
          the waters with it. The numbers read
          well. They were grooming Hillary
          but reality TV has bigger numbers.

He Laughs.

                    KAREN
          What's so funny?

                    ROMAN
          We think we're autonymous but we're
          really robots. Soap operas started
          it. Anyway - My show is going to
          prime the pump and get the message
          out. Twenty-four -- The year, not
          the TV show - is OURS.

KAREN IS BEAMING WITH PRIDE

                    KAREN
          I want to kiss you.

                    ROMAN
          What's stopping you?

SHE POURS HERSELF INTO HIS LAP - DELICIOUS MAKEOUT SESSION

FADE:

> WALTON (OC)
> Settle down you maggots.

INT. SQUAD BRIEFING ROOM (POLICE PRECINT) - DAY

Captain Walton ADDRESSES Crew.

> WALTON (CONT'D)
> You all heard about that piece of
> shit Chip Kelly.

White Cops Are SITTING With Black Cops - ALL MURMUR.

> WALTON (CONT'D)
> Pansy ass was to weak to eat a
> bullet.

> LOCKER ROOM COP
> Asshole.

Others Agree.

> WALTON
> Well they moved his trial date up.
> I'm sure the mayor had something
> to do with it. It's a political
> storm wreaking havoc at all levels.

COPS TALK

> WALTON (CONT'D)
> Of all people - Why did he have to
> be black?

LAUGHTER

> WALTON (CONT'D)
> Settle down. The mayor chewed the
> commish's ass like a piece of jerky.
> They want a strong police presence
> at the trial.

BOOS

> WALTON (CONT'D)
> (fake cough)
> I don't know - I feel a flu coming.

LAUGHTER - ALL COPS START COUGHING

INT. RUSTY'S KITCHEN - DAY

Maggie at STOVE - COOKING -- WEARS Simple (Silky) GOWN.

She DOES Have a Wonderful Butt.

HALF SLEEPING RUSTY SHUFFLES IN STARING AT HER

                    MAGGIE
          Are you staring at my ass?

                    RUSTY
          I--

                    MAGGIE
          It's okay. Sit down. Breakfast
          is ready.

SERVES HIM AT TABLE - KISSES HIS LIPS

                    RUSTY
          Maggie, you don't have to cook
          everyday. You're my guest, not
          my maid.

She HUGS Him From Behind His Chair - HANGING ON TO HIM
as She TALKS.

                    MAGGIE
          For the first time in my life, I
          feel free. I can't tell you what
          you've done for me.

                    SUZY (OC)
          Watch it sister - He's mine.

Suzy in Next to Nothing (BOY SHORTS) - PADS In Barefoot.

                    SUZY (OC)
               (to Rusty)
          How does it feel having a harem?

Maggie Laughs - Fixes Plate For Suzy.

                    RUSTY
          If anybody told me--

                    SUZY
          If anybody told me you were FBI...

                    MAGGIE
          We all have secrets.

                    SUZY
          Ain't it the truth.

                    RUSTY
          I couldn't say anything.

                    SUZY
          Trust me - I get it. The main thing
          is - It's almost over. What are
          you gonna do after? What about
          this place... And -- You know...

                    MAGGIE
          I think she means what about us.

                    RUSTY
          Look girls...

                    SUZY
          He's breaking up with us.

MAGGIE IN FAKE TEARS

                    MAGGIE
               (tears)
          I've given you the best weeks of my
          life.

ALL LAUGH

                    RUSTY
          I think we define unconventional.

                    MAGGIE
          We define inclusion.

                    SUZY
          Mags, I guess we need to start apartment
          shoppin'.

                    MAGGIE
          You should have let him kill himself.
          Then the house would have been ours.

                    SUZY
          You're a cold piece of work.

                    MAGGIE
Living with that nightmare made me
tough as nails.

                    SUZY
He changed you?

                    MAGGIE
You live with a man for thirty years
and you adopt his ways. I hate being
bias but I can't help it. I know
it's wrong - but it's ingrained.
And then to find out the thing I hate
is sleeping with me?

                    SUZY
Ain't it the truth - I know.

                    MAGGIE
I'm sorry. I forgot he was--

                    SUZY
I wish I could forget. I ain't
ever regretted a single lay until--

                    MAGGIE
It makes your skin crawl, doesn't it?

                    SUZY
Just like that movie with the--

                    RUSTY
Hello - Ladies? Remember me?

                    MAGGIE
You're still here?

LAUGHTER

                    RUSTY
Yes. And I'm going to be here permanently.
I've been promoted to section chief working
out of the L.A. office. We get to keep
this place.

Girls ATTACK Him! SMOTHER Him With KISSES...

                    RUSTY (CONT'D)
There's one more thing. Suzy, I know--

                    SUZY
I don't care what you know.
Give her some for cryin' out loud.
Can't you see the woman's in need.

                    MAGGIE
Oh, I'm fine flirting. It's fun.
I like--

                    SUZY
I'm puttin' my foot down. The three
of us are a team. Besides - I'll
feel better. I had your man, so...

                    RUSTY
Hello? Ladies. I'm right here.
Would anyone care to ask me how I--

                    SUZY/MAGGIE
Shut up.

                    MAGGIE (CONT'D)
Suzy...

                    SUZY
I insist. You got no kids, no family
but us. And who's gonna know? Fuck
'em if they can't take a joke.

                    RUSTY
Suzy. I really need to tell you--

                    SUZY
Tell me after. Let's go. Let's
go.

SHE USHERS EVERYONE TO BEDROOM

Rusty and Maggie are COMPLAINING.

                    SUZY (CONT'D)
Yeah, yeah, yeah - Whatever. Trust me.
You'll thank me after. Move it.

MAGGIES VOICE TRAILS - COMPLAINING

FADE:

INT. TV NEWS DESK - DAY

Judy ANCHORS News.

                    JUDY
          Shocking new developments in the
          Francis, Chip, Kelly case which
          gets underweigh tomorrow.

CHANGE ANGLES

          Kelly is reportedly under suicide
          watch being monitored continuously
          as he fashioned a makeshift noose
          trying to allegedly kill himself.
          We have LIVE coverage from the
          Los Angeles County jail. Lori...

EXT. L.A. COUNTY JAIL - DAY

                    LORI
          That's right Judy. Authorities
          say Chip Kelly - The infamous
          L-A-P-D officer currentlyon suspension,
          tried to commit suicide by fashioning
          a hangman's noose from several sheets
          last night.

STOCK FOOTAGE OF COUNTY JAIL

                    LORI (VO)(CONT'D)
          A deputy sheriff found Kelly fixing
          the noose around his neck - Thwarting
          his suicide attempt. He is being
          monitored in solitary isolation around
          the clock according to a deputy we spoke
          with this morning.

EXT. L.A. COUNTY JAIL - DAY

                    LORI (CONT'D)
          As you know - Officer Kelly is responsible
          for killing (19) black men single handedly.
          All shootings were ruled justifiable but
          are now being reviewed by an independent
          panel. Kelly killed (17) year old Kyle
          Lewis in May of this year, shortly after
          the now famous - George Floyd murder.

ON SCREEN:

CONTRASTING PICTURES OF CHIP

1.)   WEARING PRISTINE OFFICER'S DRESS UNIFORM

2.)   LOOKING HORRIBLE IN COUNTY JAIL JUMPSUIT

> LORI (VO)(CONT'D)
> The shocking twist of events
> happened when it was revealed by
> his estranged wife - Margaret Kelly,
> an Ancestæry dot com D-N-A test
> finding nearly twenty-percent African
> American heritage in Kelly's D-N-A.
> Judy.

SPLIT SCREEN:

JUDY AND LORI

> JUDY
> Lori, you said twenty-percent black
> blood is in Chip Kelly?

> LORI
> That's right Judy - According to a
> report I have from Ancestry dot com
> who are the leading finders of heritage
> today - Francis, Chip Kelly has nearly
> twenty-percent black blood. Here is
> a picture of his great-grandfather.

ON SCREEN:

Picture of Leroy Johson.

INT. IRISH PUB - NIGHT

All Patrons BOO LOUDLY - THROW THINGS At TV!

> BAR PATRON
> Fuckin' Kelly. I knew he was a
> weird one.

> BAR PATRON #2
> I say we go down to the courthouse
> tomorrow an' kill him!

                         BAR PATRON #3
               Killin's to kind for him. I say we
               make him suffer!

                         BAR PATRON
               Drinks on the house lads.

ALL CHEER

INT. JAIL - NIGHT

Chip is YELLING and Screaming for a PRIEST.

                         CHIP
               Get me a priest! I know my rights.
               I want a--

DOOR OPENS

Several Deputies ENTER.

                         DEPUTY
               You don't know how this works,
               do you?

                         CHIP
               Keep away from me. I'm a cop.

MEN APPROACH IN STEALTH

                         DEPUTY
               You're a piece of shit. Not
               only do you make good cops
               like us look bad...

Boys Laugh.

                         DEPUTY (CONT'D)
               You're a coon. We don't take
               kindly to coons in our house
               do we boys?

SOMEONE SPITS ON HIM

                         CHIP
               Wait! I'm tellin' you... I'm one
               of you, not one of them. I'm white!

THEY ATTACK

                         DEPUTY
              You ain't never been white, boy.

FADE:

BLACK

                         PRETTY FEMALE REPORTER (OC)
              Tensions are high outside of the
              Los Angeles Superior Court as both
              sides get ready for what promises to
              be a volatile trial.

EXT. COURTHOUSE - DAY

LORI and Her Crew in B.G. Also Reporting. News Gathering
Personnel abound.

                         PRETTY FEMALE REPORTER (CONT'D)
              Sources say officer Chip Kelly was
              beaten badly last night when a group
              of black gangsters attacked him
              enroute to the shower.

INT. COURT ROOM - DAY

Packed Full. Mostly PROTESTORS and MEDIA.

Dapper Roman with Cindy and Karen in FRONT ROW behind
Prosecutor Julie Kenoff.

Our Three PUNDITS Sit Together - RECORDING DEVICES in Hand.

Maggie (NEXT TO RUSTY WEARING HIS FBI SUIT) LOOKS Tan and
Fantastic. New (sexy) hair style. (10) years have dropped.
She HUGS Rusty's ARM as they Bring in Battered Chip
(cheap suit).

                         MAGGIE
                    (whispers)
              You should have let him do it.
              Look at him.

Chip FINDS Her With His Eyes - Smiles.

Maggie PULLS Rusty In For a Long Kiss (With TONGUE).

GIVES CHIP DISGUSTED LOOK - HE LOOKS AWAY IN SHAME

                    RUSTY
          Suzy was right. You are a cold
          piece of work.

                    MAGGIE
          I'm empowered. Where is Suzy?
          She left twenty minutes before
          we did.

                    RUSTY
          Maybe she had some precinct business.
          Where are all the cops?

NO LAPD TO BE BE FOUND - ONLY LOS ANGELES SHERIFF'S DEPUTIES

                    BALIFF
          All rise. The honorable J.P.
          Prescott, presiding.

PRESCOTT, ancient man (80s), has seen and done it all.
Little or NO Tolerance, white - MEAN.

                    PRESCOTT
          I went over the ground rules with
          counsel in my chambers. This is
          MY courtroom. I wouldn't presume
          to disrespect you in your home, I
          demand the same here. Anyone out
          of line will be placed under arrest
          and removed - No more warnings. Are
          we clear?

SOLEMN HUSH

                    PRESCOTT (CONT'D)
          Very well - Defense?

                    DEFENSE ATTORNEY
          Ready your honor.

                    PRESCOTT
          Miss Kenoff?

                    JULIE
          Ready your honor.

He NODS.

                    PRESCOTT
          Proceed.

JULIE ADDRESSES JURY

                    JULIE
          Good morning ladies and gentlemen.
          The prosecution intends to clearly
          show a pattern of reckless disregard
          for black human life over (19) --
          Excuse me - (20) shootings all
          resulting in fatalities at the hands
          of THIS MAN! A brutal, dispassionate,
          indiscriminate killer. Look at him.
          Blood lust is in his eye today just
          as it was when he gunned down an
          innocent (17) year old boy with a
          promising future... Kyle Lewis.

SITS

Defense Attorney Begins his OPENING ARGUMENT...

FADE:

INT. COURTROOM - DAY (AFTER OPEN)

                    PRESCOTT
          Call your first witness Miss Kenoff.

                    JULIE
          Thank you your honor. The prosecution
          calls undercover internal affairs LAPD
          officer - Susan Brighwell.

ALL EYES ON SUZY - WEARING DRESS UNIFORM

Maggie's Jaw DROPS to Floor!

TUGS AT RUSTY'S JACKET

                    MAGGIE
          She's...

                    RUSTY
          I know. Shh.

                    MAGGIE
          You know? How?

Suzy is SWORN IN...

Maggie is Stunned. SPEECHLESS.

                    MAGGIE (CONT'D)
          She's I-A. I thought she was--

                    RUSTY
          Shh. I can't hear her.

                    JULIE
          And in your undercover capacity did
          you in fact have occassion to interact
          with the defendant.

                    SUZY
          Several times, yes.

                    JULIE
          These interactions were of a sexual
          nature?

Suzy SOUNDS - INTELLIGENT???

                    SUZY
          Extremely sexual in nature. My job
          was to infiltrate and study certain
          questionable elements within the
          precinct, namely - officer Kelly.

                    DEFENSE ATTORNEY
          Objection your honor. This woman
          played the whore with my client.
          Personal conjugal conversations are
          protected under--

                    JULIE
          Your honor, only marital conversations
          are--

                    PRESCOTT
          I went to law school. Ojection
          overruled. Continue with the witness.

                    JULIE
          Did the defendant mention any of his
          (20) killings to you?

                    SUZY
          He mentioned each one after it happened
          in graphic detail - He bragged to me.

AUDIENCE--GASP -- PRESCOTT SCANS CROWD WITH EYES
FOR CULPRITS - SILENCE RETURNS

                    JULIE
          What exactly did he say?

                    SUZY
          After each one - His member would
          become inordinately erect...

                    JULIE
          Killing black men gave him stronger
          erections?

GASP!   SCAN -- QUIET

                    SUZY
          He would become overly animated
          while performing then - after
          his emission he would brag about
          ridding the world of another coon.

VOCAL COMMENTS

                    PRESCOTT
          You, you and you - Baliff, remove
          the prisoners. I hereby confine
          you under contempt of court.

DEAD SILENCE

JULIE SITS

                    DEFENSE ATTORNEY
          How long have you been playing the
          whore?

                    JULIE
          Your honor?

                    DEFENSE ATTORNEY
          Facts in evidence your honor.

                    PRESCOTT
          I don't like the tone but I'll allow
          it. Answer the question.

                    SUZY
          I've been undercover for all of my
          career.

                    DEFENSE ATTORNEY
          Which is how many years exactly?

                    SUZY
          I was recruitted directly from the
          academy (12) years ago.

                    DEFENSE ATTORNEY
          So, your job is to collect semen
          and information, yes?

                    JULIE
          Your honor.

                    DEFENSE ATTORNEY
          Withdrawn. How many men have you slept
          with or rather COLLECTED information
          from Miss Brightwell?

                    SUZY
          Officer Brightwell. I don't know.

                    DEFENSE ATTORNEY
          Over or under one-hundred?

SUZY LOOKS AT MAGGIE AND RUSTY IN AUDIENCE

MAGGIE IS HANGING ON TO RUSTY FOR DEAR LIFE

                    SUZY
                (slowly)
          Over.

                    DEFENSE ATTORNEY
          I see. And is it over or under (200)?

Suzy SQUIRMS in Chair.

                    DEFENSE ATTORNEY (CONT'D)
          Cat got your tongue OFFICER Brightwell?

                    SUZY
                (slowly)
          Over.

                    DEFENSE ATTORNEY
          I see. Over or under -- (500)?

Julie SEES Her Witness in Distress.

                    JULIE
          Your honor - Objection - Relevance?

DEFENSE ATTORNEY HOLDS UP FILE

                    DEFENSE ATTORNEY
          Your honor - I have here the
          record of cases this witness
          has worked on. (25) in total
          yet she has had sexual relations
          we believe with over (500) men.
          Goes to moral turpitude for
          impeachment purposes, your honor.

                    PRESCOTT
          Overruled. Answer the question.

                    SUZY
            (upset)
          If you want to know how many men
          I've had sex with...

Julie is SHAKING HER HEAD - NO!

                    DEFENSE ATTORNEY
          How many?

                    SUZY
          I stopped counting after a thousand.

                    DEFENSE ATTORNEY
          A thousand men?

Mild Uproar.

Julie is Embarassed.

                    PRESCOTT
            (points with gavel)
          Those three in the corner - And
          those two over to your right...
          Remove the prisoners!

Some People LEAVE on their OWN.

                    DEFENSE ATTORNEY
          No further questions.

                    PRESCOTT
          Step down, please.

MAGGIE INTERCEPTS HER - MAKES HER SIT DOWN NEXT TO HER

Suzy Can't Meet Rusty's Eyes.

                    JULIE
          FBI special agent Russ Ward.

LATER

                    JULIE (CONT'D)
          You were assigned uncover?

                    RUSTY
          Yes. After the nineteenth murder--

                    DEFENSE ATTORNEY
          Objection your honor. My client's
          shootings were all justified and
          cleared by several review boards.

                    PRESCOTT
          Sustained.

                    RUSTY
          After the nineteenth SHOOTING I was
          briefed on the department's undercover
          operation and assigned to covertly
          assist.

                    JULIE
          You knew about officer Brightwell?

                    RUSTY
               (looks at Suzy)
          I knew everything about officer Brightwell.
          She is a fine officer and performed her
          duty in a exemplary fashion.

                    JULIE
          Did you have occassion, if any, to
          observe the defendant shooting someone?

SILENCE

                    RUSTY
               (slowly)
          I saw that man gun down an innocent,
          unarmed black teen when I expressly told
          him not to do it. He's a KILLER!

Chip WHISPERS in Lawyer's EAR.

Julie SITS - Satisfied.

                    DEFENSE ATTORNEY
          I only have one question for this
          witness your honor. Agent Ward,
          is it true you and the defendant's
          wife are carrying on an illicit
          love affair?

MAGGIE IS ABOUT TO STAND UP - SUZY HOLDS HER DOWN!

The Courtroom is STIRRING - PRESCOTT IGNORES IT

                    PRESCOTT
          Answer the question. Are you having
          sexual intercourse with the defendant's
          wife man - Yes or no?

Rusty LOWERS His Head.

                    RUSTY
               (quietly)
          Yes.

                    PRESCOTT
          Speak up man.

MAGGIE STANDS

                    MAGGIE
          He's fucking the shit out of me
          and I'm loving every minute of it!

HUGE CROWD REACTION - CAMERAS ON AUTO

PRESCOTT MAY FALL OFF THE BENCH

                    PRESCOTT
          Remove the prisoner!

BANGS GAVEL

                    PRESCOTT
          Order! Order in this courtroom!
          Order I say! Recess - Two hours!
          We'll be closed to the media and the
          public when we return. Recess!

As the Baliffs ESCORT Smiling Chip - SPARKY (Dressed as
JANITOR) - GOES INTO MOP BUCKET - PRODUCES HANDGUN.

ROMAN SEES HIM

                    ROMAN
          Sparky - No!

SLO--MOTION

SPARKS SMILES AT HIS BROTHER - NODS HIS HEAD

TURNS TO CHIP

                    SPARKY
          Two for one - nigga.

SHOOTS HIM REPEATEDLY

SETS HIS GUN ON GROUND - SMILING AT ROMAN

DEPUTIES OPEN FIRE ---

BLACK FEMALE GOSPEL SINGER - HUMS MOURNFUL RIFF

                    ROMAN
          No!

Cindy and Karen BLOCK Him From Running to Sparky.

HE BREAKS FREE - SPARKY SMILES AS HE DIES IN HIS HANDS

                    SPARKY
          I got him. I got him.

ROMAN ROCKS HIS LIFELESS BODY BACK AND FORTH - CRYING

KISSES HIS BROTHER'S FOREHEAD

                    ROMAN
          I love you Sparky - I love you.

VARIOUS REACTIONS

FADE OUT:

                    THE END

SILENCE

BLACK

                    SPARKY (OC)
          Hey Roman bread...
                    (MORE)

FIZZLE IN:

ON SCREEN:

SPARKY HAS RECORDED HIMSELF ON CELL PHONE

                    SPARKY (CONT'D)
          If you're lookin' at this that means
          I'm dead, but I got his ass too.
          Look here bro' - When you beat Chuckie
          Walter's ass for me back in the day,
          I realized then - I ain't the big
          brother you need. I ain't shit.

LOOKS TO DISTANT OBJECT - BACK AT CAMERA

          And that's okay. All of us can't be
          you. You're special. You see what
          needs to be done and you do it. Mama
          knew. Look here bro' - Maybe I was
          born for one thing - to rid this earth
          of that man. I don't mind dyin'.
          I goin' home with mama and Reggie and
          Junior.

LOOK AWAY AGAIN - THINKING

          I'm sorry to leave you alone down here.
          At least now you ain't gotta be the
          head of the family no more. Make some
          movies. Don't let all our deaths be
          for nothin' please. God has a plan and
          that plan is you bro'. Do the right thing.

FIZZLES:

COMES BACK ON

                    SPARKY (CONT'D)
          Oh! And I KNOW mama bought you that
          pie you tried to sneak all on your own.
          Wish I had boxin' skills. Later bro'.
          Oh yeah, I love you.

FIZZLE:

FADE TO BLACK.

ROLL END CREDITS

Please Order Your Copy Of:

FROM PROTEST TO POLICY

by

Prince Maryland

Available at: amazon.com

"For a dream cometh through the multitude of business..."

Ecclesiastes - 5:3

"Trigger Happy" 2nd draft.   Copyright July 15, 2020.
All rights reserved by author. (Original story & screenplay
written by - Prince Maryland)

Contact:

PrinceMaryland@PriorMilitaryProductions.com

Write directly to:

Prince Maryland - F86550
PO Box 705
Soledad, CA 93960
CTF - Facility B - SA/255 Low

Protests raise awareness. The entire world is AWARE of
the BLM and the problem. Conversations are worthless without
corresponding action. The time to ACT is now.

This movie is an EXCELLENT Step in the right direction.
I would ask you to help make it a reality, please - Thank You!

PS The 1st draft of Trigger Happy is included in the
    book "From Protest to Policy" I think you will enjoy
    both versions.

FINALLY

Thank you for enduring this typewriter which is on its
very last leg. Talk about challenges - Can someone PLEASE
put this in FINAL DRAFT for me???